KU-466-170

Penguin Modern European Poets
Advisory Editor: A. Alvarez

Selected Poems: Cesare Pavese

Cesare Pavese, novelist and poet, was born in
Piedmont in 1908, the son of a judiciary
official in Turin. He was educated at Turin,
took a literature degree with a thesis on
Walt Whitman, and later became a
schoolmaster. In 1930 he began to contribute
essays on American literature to *La Cultura*, of
which he became editor in 1934. At the same
time he began translations of English and
American writers (Defoe, Dickens, Joyce,
Melville, Stein, and Faulkner), whose works
exerted considerable influence not only on his
own narrative style, but also on that of other
Italian novelists. In 1935 he was arrested for
anti-fascist activities and sentenced to
preventive detention at the lonely seashore
prison of Brancaleone, and it was this
experience which became the basis of his novel
The Political Prisoner (*Il carcere*). Between 1936
and 1940 nine of his books were published in
Italy: these included novels, short stories,
poetry, and essays. Two novels, *The Moon and
the Bonfire* and *The Devil in the Hills* are also
available in Penguins. In 1950 Pavese
committed suicide.

Selected Poems

Cesare Pavese

*Edited, translated and
with a Foreword by*
Margaret Crosland

 Penguin Books

Penguin Books Ltd, Harmondsworth,
Middlesex, England
Penguin Books Australia Ltd, Ringwood,
Victoria, Australia

First published in English under the title *A Mania for Solitude*,
Selected Poems 1930–1950, by Peter Owen 1969
Published in Penguin Books 1971

Copyright © Giulio Einaudi Editore S.p.A., 1962
Translations copyright © Peter Owen Ltd, 1969

Made and printed in Great Britain by
Richard Clay (The Chaucer Press) Ltd,
Bungay, Suffolk
Set in Monotype Bembo

This book is sold subject to the condition that
it shall not, by way of trade or otherwise, be lent,
re-sold, hired out, or otherwise circulated without
the publisher's prior consent in any form of
binding or cover other than that in which it is
published and without a similar condition
including this condition being imposed on the
subsequent purchaser

Contents

Foreword

Cesare Pavese was one of the outstanding young Italian writers of the mid 1930s who were committed to the political left wing and imprisoned by the fascist authorities for their activities and writings. His first mature collection of poetry, *Lavorare stanca*, was published in 1936 under the auspices of the literary review *Solaria* and comprised forty-five poems.

After his release from prison in 1936 Pavese joined the Einaudi publishing firm in Turin and continued to write stories and novels, which have been translated into English with great success. He also translated books by well-known English and American writers into Italian and wrote perceptive essays about them.

In 1943 Einaudi published an augmented version of *Lavorare stanca*, to which Pavese contributed two essays, *Il mestiere di poeta* (The Poet's Craft) and *A proposito di certe poesie non ancora scritte* (Concerning Certain Poems Not Yet Written), which appeared as an appendix. The seventy poems in this famous collection – whose sequence had been arranged by Pavese himself in 1940 – have a narrative content: they are about people living in the Piedmontese countryside and in Turin. Many of the poems were drawn from Pavese's childhood memories of his country birthplace; others are about city life and its problems – adolescents who run away from home, prostitutes who accept life as it is, men who are out of work. There are various lonely figures in these poems, but clearly the loneliest of all was Pavese himself, an impression corroborated by his moving diary, *Il mestiere di vivere* (This Business of Living), which he started while in prison at Brancaleone in 1935 and continued until his suicide in 1950, when he was only forty-two.

In 1947 a group of nine poems, *La terra e la morte* (Earth and Death), appeared in the review *Le tre Venezie* (Padua), and these poems were included in the volume *Verrà la morte e avrà i tuoi occhi* (Death Shall Come, Using Your Eyes), published posthumously in 1951. They were reprinted also in an anthology of modern Italian poetry which came out in 1950, edited by Giacinto Spagnoletti and titled *Antologia della poesia italiana 1909–1949*.

The present selection has been made from the 1962 edition of *Lavorare stanca*, published by Einaudi. Edited by Italo Calvino, that edition includes all Pavese's known poems, apart from juvenilia, together with an appendix comprising the two essays which had originally been printed in the 1943 edition. These essays, the second of which Pavese considered as his conclusive statement on his poetry, appear at the beginning of this English selection. The notes that follow the translated poems are based mainly on those written by Italo Calvino for the Einaudi collection of 1962. The poems themselves are given in the same chronological sequence as the 1962 Italian edition, and their dates of composition have been taken from Calvino's notes.

The many admirers of Pavese's novels and other writings will find here most of the poems mentioned in *This Business of Living*. They are an essential complement to his prose work and express more clearly than his other writings Pavese's nostalgia for country life and childhood, his awareness of social change and his deep understanding of people as isolated as himself. These poems are about Italy, but the situations and attitudes they convey epitomize human characteristics and values that are universal. By the end of the 1930s Pavese had realized that he could no longer write the short narrative poems for which he had consciously developed an individual technique. During the last few years of his life he published three sequences of lyric poems, different from all his earlier writing but equally compelling through their haunting evocation of love, which for Pavese was inexorably linked with tragedy.

I should like to thank Mrs Nuccia Foulkes and Sig. Michele Spina for the help they have given me in preparing this translation, and Mr Michael Levien who has been a most patient and constructive editor.

MARGARET CROSLAND

Note to the Penguin Edition

For this Penguin edition of Pavese's poems, certain revisions have been made.

M.C.

Author's Note

As an appendix to the definitive edition of this book of mine (which integrates and replaces the first edition of 1936), I am adding two studies in which I attempted successively to clarify for myself its significance and expression. The first, *The Poet's Craft*, I wrote in November 1934, and its interest for me now is purely documentary. Almost all the affirmations and lofty statements are amended and superseded by the second, *Concerning Certain Poems Not Yet Written*, composed in 1940. Whatever my future as a writer may be, I regard the searchings of *Lavorare stanca* as concluded with this piece of prose.

CESARE PAVESE

1 *The Poet's Craft*

The composition of this collection lasted three years. Three years of youth and discovery, during which my own ideas about poetry and my intuitive capacities naturally became deeper. And even now, although I can see that this depth and strength have faded to a great extent, I do not believe that all, absolutely all my life has been pinned down in emptiness. I may or may not make other attempts at poetry, I shall concern myself with other things or I shall even reduce every experience to this end: I want to set aside everything that has preoccupied me so far. Simply, I have here a body of work which concerns me, not so much because it was composed by me but rather because for a time at least I believed it to be the best that was being written in Italy and because then as now I am the man best equipped to understand it.

Instead of this natural evolution from one type of poetry to another, which I have mentioned, others would prefer to discover in this collection what is called a construction, that is a hierarchy of moments expressing some concept, great or small, through its abstract, even esoteric nature, and thus revealed in tangible forms. Now I do not deny that some of these concepts can be discovered in my collection, but I do deny vehemently that I put them there.

Let me make myself clear: I myself have been made thoughtful by real or presumed constructed lyrics (*Les fleurs du mal* or *Leaves of Grass*), I will even say that I came to envy them through their vaunted quality; but in the end, in my attempt to understand them and justify them to myself, I have had to accept that between one type of poetry and another there is no imaginative progress and not even any conceptual progress. At the most, as in *Halcyon Days*, there is a temporal link, images going from June to September. Naturally I would feel differently about a narrative or a poem, where the passage that is simultaneously imaginative and conceptual is produced by the narrative element, that is by the consciousness of an ideal and material unity which brings together the various moments of an experience. But then one must renounce the pretence of constructing simply by the juxtaposition of unities: one must have the courage and strength to conceive a major work all of a piece. Just as two poems do not form a single narrative (at the most they contain links of kinship between the respective characters or similar elements), two or more poems do not form a story or a construction, except on the understanding that each one is not complete on its own. It should satisfy our ambition, and in this collection it satisfies mine, that within its brief compass each poem succeeds in being a self-contained construction.

All this appears fairly elementary but – I do not know whether it is through my personal ingenuity or through a type of poetic taste currently in the air – it is precisely in a long work concerning this identity – each poem is a story – that all the attempts included in this book are technically justified.

I searched in a confused way for an essential expression of essential facts, but not the usual introspective abstraction expressed in that type of language which is unsatisfactory because it is bookish, allusive, and claims too gratuitously to be essential. Now, the false lyric poem achieves precisely the illusion of a construction through the links that one page provides with another by means of the evanescence of its voices and the significance of its motifs.

In order to follow my own taste and not lapse into lyric poetry I incurred demands in two ways, in the first place the demand of technique because of the respect I had always had for it, but naturally all my faculties were engaged.

At the same time one of my ideas about the poem as story, which at first I had not successfully distinguished from the short poem, was taking shape within me. Naturally it is not only a question of form. The reserves described by Poe, which are still valid, about the concept of the poem, are now integrated with considerations of content, which then form one entity only with these external considerations on the structure of one component. It was here that at first I did not see clearly, and thus with some effrontery flattered myself I had achieved a sufficiently strong act of faith in poetry which I know to be clear and distinct, muscular, objective, essential and so forth. I was speaking in principle about evolution. And this is precisely where evolution lies: in the growing awareness of this problem, which in my poetry seems to me even today to be anything but exhausted.

The first notable product of this vain aspiration is in fact the first poem in the collection: 'The South Seas'. But it goes without saying that from the first day that I thought of a poem, I struggled with the presentiment of this difficulty. Endless attempts at poems preceded 'The South Seas', and simultaneous experience in writing narrative or merely discursive prose removed all joy of achievement from them, revealing their desperate banality.

I passed sharply from a form of lyricism that lay between ecstatic outpouring and deep probing (unsuccessful probing that often became an unjustifiable and vicious outpouring which always ended in a pathological scream) to the calm and clear narrative of 'The South Seas'; I explained this to myself simply by remembering that it did not happen all at once, but for almost a year before 'The South Seas' I had thought seriously of writing poetry. In the meantime, as previously but with greater intensity, I was occupied on the one hand with the study and translation of North American literature, while on the other I was producing short stories half in dialect and, in collaboration with a painter friend, an amateur collection of pornography of which I need say no more here. It need only be mentioned that this pornographic collection resulted in a group of ballads, tragedies, lyrics and poems in octaves, all vigorously Sotadic in style, but this is of little consequence now. What does matter is that the work was conceived and narrated with gaiety and vigour, aimed at a public of friends and very much appreciated by some of them; the practical motivation was the existence of a public, which seems to me to act like fertilizer on the roots of all flourishing artistic vegetation.

The connection between these occupations and 'The South Seas' is therefore complex: the studies in North American literature placed me in contact with a growing cultural reality, the attempts at short-story writing brought me closer to a better human experience and objectivized its themes; and finally my third occupation, from the technical angle, revealed to me the professionalism of art and the joy of overcoming difficulties, the limits of a theme, the play of imagination and style, and the mystery of what makes a felicitous style, which also means reckoning with the possible listener or reader. And I insist especially on the technical lesson of this last activity of mine, for the other influences, North American culture and human experience, are too easily understood within the single concept of experience which explains everything and therefore nothing.

Further, in a more subtly technical manner the three activities that I have described influenced the convictions, intentions and data with which I began 'The South Seas'. In each of the three cases I entered variously into contact with the development of a linguistic creation based on dialect or at least on the spoken word. I mean by this the discovery during my studies of North American popular speech and the use of Turin or Piedmontese slang in my attempts at naturalistic prose dialogue. Both activities were enthusiastic, youthful adventures, serving as a basis for more than one thought which quickly evaporated and became integrated through the encounter with the identifying theory of poetry and language.

In the third place the constant parody-type style of Sotadic versification accustomed me to consider all kinds of literary language as a dead, crystallized body, in which there could be no circulation of blood and no life without the transposition and grafting of spoken, technical and dialect words. And this threefold, unique experience continually showed me, through the confused way in which I distributed these various expressive and practical interests, the fundamental interdependence of these motifs and the need for a continual re-examination of principles, in order to avoid impoverishment. This prepared me for the idea that the condition of every poetic impulse, however lofty, is always an attempt to meet ethical demands, and also, naturally, the practical demands of surroundings in which one lives.

'The South Seas', which came after this natural preparation, is therefore my first attempt at a narrative poem and justifies this twofold condition as an objective development of situations, set out in a *straightforward* and therefore, I thought, imaginative way. But the important point is in the *objectivity* of the sequence of incidents, a fact which reduces my attempt to a little poem somewhere between the psychological and the narrative; however, it develops on a naturalistic theme. I insisted at that time on a straightforward style as a fundamental polemical position: it was a question of acquiring imaginative evidence outside *all the* *other* expressive attitudes which seemed to me corrupted by rhetoric; it was a question of proving to myself that straightforward energy in the conception carried within itself the closely associated, immediate and essential expression. Nothing was more ingenuous than my contention at that time about the *image* regarded in the rhetorical sense: I did not want images in my poetry and I did not put any there, unless by accident. This was in order to preserve the immediacy I wanted so much and, by taking a risk, to avoid the facile and sloppy lyricism of the *imaginifici* (I overdid it).*

It is natural that with such a programme of simplicity salvation can only be found in close, possessive and passionate adherence to the object. And it is perhaps only the strength of this passion and not objective straightforwardness which saves something in these first poems. Soon I felt the impact of the argument or of the object, which was inevitable in such a materialistic conception of narrative. I often found myself pondering over arguments, and this was a good thing: I still do so to undeniable advantage. The thing that does not work is to seek an argument while being inclined to let it develop according to its psychological or narrative nature and accept the results. Or to identify oneself with this element and passively allow its laws to act. This means yielding to the object. And this is what I did.

But although the anxiety engendered by a mistake of this kind did not leave me even then, it did give me a means of satisfaction. Above all, the *objective style* gave me some consolation through its solid honesty: its incisive form and the clear-cut accent that I still envy. It was also accompanied by a certain sentimental touch of misogynous virility which

* The 'image-makers', a word used to describe the writer D'Annunzio and his followers. M.C.

I liked and which definitely, with certain other accompanying touches, formed the real theme, the real *development of situations* in my narrative poems, which I imagined to be objective. Then, thank goodness, if theories are often good and achievements poor, sometimes the reverse is true. And in fact after years of evanescent shrill poems, I succeeded in making one of my poems smile – a figure in a poem – and this seemed to me tangible proof that style had been conquered and experience overcome.

I had also created a personal kind of verse, which I swear I did not do deliberately. At that time I knew only that free verse did not suit me very well, because of its capricious and undisciplined exaggerations that usually pass for imagination. I have written elsewhere of the free verse of Whitman, which on the contrary I greatly admired and feared, describing my confused presentiment that so much rhetoric demanded inspiration to bring it to life. I lacked both the inspiration and temperament to use it. I had no faith in traditional metres because of the amount of triteness and unjustified fiddling about which I thought they implied: and, moreover, I had used them too much in parody for me to take them seriously and achieve a rhyming effect which would not strike me as comic.

I knew naturally that there are no traditional metres in the absolute sense, but every poet re-creates in himself the interior rhythms of his imagination. And I found myself one day mumbling a certain long string of words (which later became a distich in 'The South Seas') to a pompous rhythm which I had adopted ever since reading novels as a boy, murmuring over and over again the phrases which obsessed me. In this way, without knowing it, I had found my kind of verse which in 'The South Seas' and for several other poems was solely instinctive (traces of this unconscious use remain in some of the first lines, which are no different from traditional hendecasyllables). I worked out the rhythms of my poetry by repeating them to myself. Gradually I discovered the intrinsic laws of this metre and the hendecasyllables disappeared; my verse fell into three unvarying categories, which in a certain way I could work out before the composition, but I was always careful not to be tyrannized and was ready to accept, when it seemed necessary, other accents and other syllabification. But I did not depart much further from my scheme and I regard this as the rhythm of my imagination.

It is superfluous now for me to say how good I consider this type of versification to be. It is enough to say that it suited also my material requirement, which was completely intuitive, for long lines, because I felt I had a lot to say and should not confine myself to musical justification for my verses but satisfy also their logic. This was successful, and for better or worse, I gave them *narrative*.

This is the major point under examination. I wrote narrative, but how? I have already said that I regard the first in the collection as factual little poems about which it can charitably be said that the *facts* constitute no more than obstacles, a residue unresolved in the imagination. I imagined a situation or a character and I made them develop or speak. In order not to lapse into writing 'little poems', which in a confused way I felt to be wrong, I exerted a miserly economy over the writing of lines, setting a limit for each poem in advance. All the same, it seemed important that there should not be too few, for I was nervous of producing epigrams. Such is the drawback of an education in rhetoric. At this juncture too I was saved by a certain calm and by an interest in other things of the mind and in life, which not only contributed something but allowed me to meditate *ex novo* on the problems, distracting me from the ferocious zeal with which I applied to all my inventive and whimsical aspiration the demands of the *virile objectivity* in the story. As for the literary side, a new interest was my violent passion for Shakespeare and other Elizabethans, all of whom I had read and annotated, and they remained in my head.

One day I wanted to write a poem about a hermit whom I had imagined, a poem in which the motives and methods of his conversion would be described. I realized that I had not succeeded in expressing myself and by means of endless polishing, rewriting, changes of mind, self-criticism and anxiety, I put together instead a 'Landscape',* including the high and low parts of a hill which were contrasted and full of movement. The central animator of this scheme was a hermit standing and lying down, a superior kind of joker and, despite my anti-image-making convictions, his colour was 'the same as the scorched ferns'. The very words I have used make it clear that the basis of my imagination in this instance is a pictorial emotion; and in fact before writing 'Landscape' I had seen and envied some new pictures by my painter friend, which revealed astonishing colour and knowledge of construction. But whatever the stimulus, the novelty of this attempt is now quite clear to me: I had discovered the *image*.

I find it difficult at this point to explain myself, because I have not exhausted the possibilities implicit in the technique of 'Landscape'. I had therefore discovered the value of the image, and – this was the reward for the obstinacy with which I had insisted on the objectivity of the narrative – I no longer saw it in a rhetorical sense as metaphoric, as a more or less arbitrary decoration superimposed on the objectivity of the narrative. This image was in an obscure way the narrative itself.

* 'Landscape I', p. 50. M.C.

The fact that the hermit appeared to be the colour of the scorched ferns did not mean that I was drawing a parallel between the hermit and the ferns in order to bring out either the hermit or the ferns. It meant that I had discovered an *imaginative relationship* between hermit and ferns, between hermit and landscape (I could go on: between hermit and girls, between visitors and peasants, between girls and vegetation, between hermit and goat, between hermit and excrement, between the high and low parts of the hill), *which was itself the theme of the narrative*.

I told the story of this relationship, regarding it as a significant whole, created from the imagination and full of imaginative seeds capable of development; and in the clarity of this imaginative complex and also in its possibility of infinite development, I saw the *reality* of the composition. (The mania for objectivity, which now clarified itself as a need for concreteness, had been transformed to this plane.)

I had gone back (or so I thought) to the source of all poetic activity, which I could have defined as follows: the power to render as a self-sufficient whole a complex of imaginative relationships, in which is embodied the true perception of a reality. I continued to scorn and avoid the image as understood in the rhetorical sense and my writing remained continually direct and objective (objective, that is, in the new sense), although ultimately I could say I possessed the extremely elusive understanding of that simple enunciation that the essence of poetry is the imagery. I had encountered plenty of formal images in the rhetorical sense, in scenes by the Elizabethan dramatists, but precisely at this time I was laboriously persuading myself that their importance lay not so much in the rhetorical significance of terms of comparison but rather in my interpretation, which I had finally perceived, of the parts essential to a total imaginative reality, whose meaning lay in their relationship. This discovery was favoured by the peculiar nature of the Elizabethan image, so overflowing with life, so ingenious, and satisfied with its own ingeniousness and richness as its own ultimate justification. For this reason many scenes from those dramas appeared to me to draw their imaginative inspiration exclusively from the atmosphere created by their resemblance to each other.

The history of what I composed after the first 'Landscape' is naturally, at first, the history of lapses into the earlier objectivity, psychological or narrative. This is the case for instance in 'People Who Don't Understand', although the whole poem is permeated with new elements. Later it became almost a matter of course for me to translate into imaginary terms each motif of experience, and the process became constantly more assured and instinctive. It was at this point that I became aware of a new problem, which I have not yet solved.

It is all very well, I would say, to substitute for the objective data an imaginary narrative with a more concrete and well-informed reality; but where should this search for imaginative relationships end? That is, how can one justify the choice of one relationship more than another? I became uneasy, in a poem like 'A Mania for Solitude', about the bold pre-eminence of the I (which it had been my policy from the time of 'The South Seas' to reduce to a subordinate character and sometimes abolish), not so much intending it as an objective argument, which was a childish fear, but more because I believed that the pre-eminence of the I was accompanied by a more disordered interplay of the imaginative relationships. When, in fact, does imaginative power become the arbiter? My definition of the image did not enlighten me on this question.

I have still not solved this difficulty. It still exists for me because it is the critical point of all poetic art. I perceive a possible solution, yet it does not really satisfy me because it is not very clear. Nevertheless, I regard it as having a certain value, since it brings me back to that conviction of the fundamental interdependence of practical and expressive motifs, of which I spoke in connection with my development from the point of view of language. The criterion of what is opportune, in the play of the imagination, would lie in a *reasonable* closeness to that logical and moral complex which constitutes personal participation in reality in its spiritual sense. It goes without saying that this participation is always mutable and renewable, and as a result its imaginative effect can be incarnated in an infinite number of situations. But the weakness of the definition results from that reasonableness which is so necessary and so inconclusive in so far as the effects of judgement on the work are concerned. Must we then affirm the precariousness and superficiality of all aesthetic judgement? We might be tempted to do so.

In the meantime I worked in a state of creative frenzy, and always battling in various ways with the same difficulty. I put together other narratives made up of images. By this time I even enjoyed taking technical risks. In 'Nocturnal Pleasures', for example, I wanted to construct a relationship, by contrast, of sensuous reactions, and without lapsing into sensuality. In 'Building a House' the play of images is concealed within an apparently objective narrative. In 'Sad Supper' I relate a trite situation in my own manner, by introducing imaginative relationships.

Through each of these poems I experienced again the anxiety caused by the problem of how to understand and justify the imaginative complex of which it consisted. I became continually more adept at suggestion, subdued tones and rich composition, and continually less convinced of the honesty and *necessity* of my work. When I compared my poems, sometimes the spare and almost prosaic verse of 'The South Seas' or 'Deola' seemed to me more justified than the vivid, flexible line, full of imaginative life, to be found for example in 'Portrait of the Author' and other poems. But I remained faithful to the clearly defined principle: the straightforward and direct expression of a clearly perceived imaginative relationship. I wanted to tell a story and not lose myself in unnecessary frills. But it is a fact that my images – my imaginative relationships – became continually more complicated and branched out into rarefied atmospheres.

2 Concerning Certain Poems Not Yet Written

One fact must be observed: after a certain silence one proposes to write not *a poem* but *poems*. One regards the future page as a dangerous exploration of something one will soon know how to tackle. Words, form, situations, rhythms of tomorrow morning promise us a wider background than the single piece that we will write.

If this broadening process in the future should lack horizon, and thereby merge with our possible future in its *entirety*, the normal urge would be to preserve oneself and work hard, and that's all. But a certain spiritual dimension or duration is implicit within it, and as a result the limits present in the same internal logic of the new thing we are creating cannot be seen. The poetry we are in the process of writing will open those doors on to our capacity for creative work, and we will go through those doors – we will write other poems, will strip the field of its fruit and leave it bare. This is the essential point: the limitation, that is the dimension, of the new province. The poem we will write tomorrow will open some doors to us, not all possible ones: a moment will come, that is, when we will write 'tired' poems, empty of promise, poems in fact that will indicate the end of the adventure. But if the adventure has a beginning and an end, it means that the poems composed within it form a bloc and constitute the body of lyric poems of which we had been afraid.

It is not easy to realize when such an adventure ends, given the fact that the 'tired' poems, or conclusion poems, are perhaps the finest of the group, and the tedium that accompanies their composition is not great but different from that which opens a new horizon. For example, I composed 'Simplicity' and 'The Morning Star' (winter 1935-6) with indescribable boredom, and perhaps precisely in order to escape from this boredom, treated them in a way so daring and allusive that on reading them again later they seem full of promise. The psychological criterion of tedium is not therefore sufficient to indicate that a step has been taken towards a new group, given that boredom and dissatisfaction are the starting-point of some poetic discovery, small or great.

A more reliable criterion is that of *intention*. Our poems are defined as 'tired' and coming to an end, or at the start of something rich in development, because we ourselves decide to consider them so. Obviously this criterion is not arbitrary, since it will never occur to us to dictate the meaning of a poem in a capricious way; we will choose to develop not those which appeared to have promise when we composed them (this would be very rare, because of the boredom mentioned above), but those which, when we think them over after composition, offer us positive hopes for later compositions. At the same time it must be said that the unity of a group of poems (the poem) is not an abstract concept to be put down in draft form, but an organic circulation of pretexts and meanings which is gradually determined in concrete form. What happens therefore is that, when the whole group is composed, its unity will not yet be evident to you and you will have to discover it by dissecting each poem separately, rearranging the poems in a different order and understanding them better. By this process the material unity of a narrative is achieved as it were by itself, and it is a naturalistic thing for the very mechanism of the narrative.

I have excluded the fact that the construction of the new

group can have an autobiographical plan, which would be narration in its naturalistic meaning.

I had then to decide whether certain isolated poems (not including those from the first *Lavorare stanca*) were the conclusion of an old group and the start of a new one. The fact that in composing them I had the intention of going beyond *Lavorare stanca* was due only to a minor extent to the fact that the book was already with the printer. The winter of 1935-6 marked the crisis of a whole mood of optimism based on old habits and the start of new thinking about my craft, which was expressed in a diary and developed gradually into a deepening of my inner life through prose, and through successive preoccupations (1937-9) which induced me to try writing short stories and novels. Occasionally I wrote a poem – the winter of 1937-8 produced several during a return to the conditions of 1934, the year of *Lavorare stanca* – but I became continually more convinced that my actual field was prose, and the poems represented an *afterglow*.* Then in 1939 there were no more. Then, with the beginning of 1940, I went back to them and wondered whether these extra ones fitted into *Lavorare stanca* or gave some indication of the future.

The fact remains that when I picked up the book again and rearranged it in order to include some poems which had been censored in 1935, the new ones fell into place easily and seemed to form a whole. The question was therefore resolved in a practical manner, but the fact remained that the *direction* of the extra poems gave me distinct hope of a new body of poetry.

Let us see. These extra poems fall into two groups, also chronological. Winter 1935-6, the end of imprisonment: 'Myth', 'Simplicity', 'The Morning Star'; winter 1937-8,

* In English in the original. M.C.

sexual passion: 'The Country Whore', 'The Drunken Old Woman', 'The Boatman's Wife'. It is clear that these two moments are already included in *Lavorare stanca*; the first group is recognizable in 'Poggio Reale', the second in 'Sad Supper' and 'Motherhood'. The important question is whether something in their accent justifies the intention of including them in a future collection, as I had certainly hoped when I composed them.

This does not seem to be the case. The novelty of 'The Morning Star' is only on the surface. The sea, the mountain and the star, the solitary man, are elements or imaginative concepts which already occur in 'Away from Home', 'A Mania for Solitude' and 'Ulysses'. Neither is the rhythm of the imaginative treatment different or even richer than in the past. The human figure seen through his essential gestures and through this narrative does not emerge. The same can be said of the portraits of women in the second group ('The Drunken Old Woman' and 'The Boatman's Wife') which, aside from the totally external part played by dream, repeat the figurative presentation of 'Ulysses' and other poems, having recourse to the internal image (a detail of the picture, used as a means of comparison in the narrative) and not even achieving the nebulous ideal of the image-narrative put forward in 1934. At the same time the restrained treatment of 'The Boatman's Wife' takes us straight back to 'Deola'.

The truth of the matter is that during these years constructive intention was expressed more in the diary meditations which accompanied the poetry and finally burnt out (1937–9). And since only critical awareness concludes a poetic cycle, this continual insistence with notes in prose on the problem of my verses is the proof that a further crisis of renewal was imminent. We will say therefore that if in the work I succeeded gradually in defining *Lavorare stanca* to myself, so much so that in the end I took it up again and rearranged it, discovering a construction in it (something which in 1934 I found absurd), I aimed to go further. An examination of the poetics of the extraneous groups showed that the style fitted coherently into the rest of *Lavorare stanca*, proving the vain hope of a new poetic art and outlining the direction it was taking. What then was the reason for those repeated and fragmentary questionings in prose which occupied me for three years?

Lavorare stanca can be defined as the adventure of the adolescent boy who is proud of the countryside where he lives and imagines that the city will resemble it, but he finds solitude in the city and remedies it with sex and passion which only succeed in uprooting him and leaving him far from country and town, in a more tragic solitude which is the end of adolescence. I had discovered in this collection of poems a formal coherence which is the evocation of figures that are all solitary but alive in the imagination, inasmuch as they are firmly attached to their short-lived world by means of the *internal image*. (Example: In the last 'Landscape'* with the mist, the air is intoxicating, the beggar breathes it in as he breathes in the grappa, the boy drinks in the morning. This is the whole imaginative life of *Lavorare stanca*.)

Now the adventure that was lived through during these four years and its evocative technique are past. The former ended with the practical acceptance and justification of masculine solitude, the latter with a few attempts at new rhythms and types of figuration. Rightly, my criticism concentrated most of all on the concept of the image. The ambitious definition of 1934, that the image itself was the theme of the narrative, was revealed as false or at least

* 'Landscape VI'. M.C.

premature. Since then I have evoked real figures, rooting them to their background by means of internal comparisons, but this comparison has never been the theme of the narrative, for the reason that the theme was a person, or a landscape understood in a naturalistic way. It is not the case after all that I had foreseen the possible unity of *Lavorare stanca* only in the form of a naturalistic adventure. Each poem has the same characteristics as the collection as a whole.

Let it be said clearly: my adventure of tomorrow should have other motivations.

This new collection of poems will have its own explanation when it is written; that is, when I shall be obliged to reject it. But two premises emerge from this: (1) its construction will be similar to that of each single poem; (2) it will not be possible to express it in a naturalistic narrative.

The unnecessary element – the demands of a type of poetry which cannot be reduced to narrative – is, all the same, the leaven for tomorrow. It is the arbitrary, pre-critical element which alone can stimulate creation. It is an intention, an irrational premise, which will be justified only by the work. Four years of vain aspirations and introspection impose it on me, just as during 1931–2 a voice forced me to *narrate* verses.

It is logical that in the face of this demand there appears the other inconclusive demand, that of knowing what the new poetry will say. The poetry itself will say this, and when it has said it, it will be a thing of the past, as *Lavorare stanca* is now.

It is certain that once again the problem of the image will dominate the situation. But it will not be a question of *narrating images*, an empty formula, as we have seen, because nothing can distinguish the words which evoke an image from those which evoke an object. It will be a question of describing – whether directly or by means of images is immaterial – a reality which is not naturalistic but symbolic. In these poems the facts will speak – if they speak – not because reality wishes it but because intelligence decides it will be so. Individual poems and the whole body of poems will not be an autobiography but a judgement. As it happens in *La divina commedia* (we had to reach this point) – a warning that my symbol will want to correspond not to Dante's allegory but to his images.

There will be no point in thinking of the collection of poems. As we have seen with *Lavorare stanca* it will be necessary from time to time to absorb oneself in the individual poem and by this to overcome the past. If the first of the two axioms is correct, it will be enough to write one single new poem – perhaps this has already been done – and the entire collection of poems will be safe. Not only this, but given one verse all will be implicit in it. A day will come when a tranquil glance will bring order and unity into the arduous chaos which starts tomorrow.

The South Seas

To Augusto Monti

One evening we walked along the side of a hill
in silence. In the late evening dusk
my cousin was a giant dressed in white
with a bronzed face, he moved quietly,
silently. Silence is our strength.
One of us was surely often alone –
some great man among half-wits or a poor lunatic –
to teach so much silence to his family.

My cousin talked this evening. He asked
me to climb with him: from the top, on a clear night,
you can see the distant light,
the glow of Turin. 'You who live in Turin . . .'
he said to me '. . . but you're right. You must live
a long way from home, make good, enjoy yourself
and then come back at forty, like me,
everything's new. The Langhe hills don't disappear.'
He told me all this, he didn't speak Italian,
but talked slowly in dialect, the speech that's as rugged
as the stones of the hill,
and twenty years of other words and seas
had not scratched it. And he walked along the slope
with the set expression that I used to see
on tired peasant faces when I was a child.

He spent twenty years travelling the world.
I was still a baby when he went away,
and they said he was dead. Then I heard the women
mention him sometimes, like a legend;
but the men, who were more serious, forgot him.

One winter a postcard came for my father, who was
    already dead;
it had a big green stamp with ships in port
and sent best wishes for the wine harvest. They were all
    amazed,
but I had grown up now, I could explain
that the message came from an island called Tasmania
ringed with bluer seas, where the sharks were fierce,
in the Pacific, south of Australia. I added that
my cousin was surely fishing for pearls. And I took off the
    stamp.
They all made bets, but everyone thought
that if he weren't dead, he'd die.
Then they all forgot and much time passed.

Oh how long since I played at Malayan pirates,
how much time has gone by. And since I last
went down to bathe at a dangerous place
and followed a playmate under a tree,
parted the branches and split open
a rival's head and someone shot me,
how much life has gone by. Other days, other games,
other shedding of blood before rivals
more elusive: thoughts and dreams.
The city has taught me endless fear:
a crowd, a street, sometimes a thought observed on a face,
have made me tremble.
I can still feel, still see the mocking light
of thousands of street-lamps above the trampling feet.

My cousin came back, his struggles over,
like a giant among the few. And he had money.
'Within a year at most,' said his parents quietly,
'if he's spent it all he'll return to his travels.

The hopeless wander like that.'
There's a scar on my cousin's face. He bought a plot of land
nearby and had a concrete garage built
with a bright light outside, for selling petrol,
and a big poster on the curving bridge.
Then he brought in a mechanic to take the money
and walked all over the Langhe hills, smoking.
In the meantime he married, locally. He chose a girl
slim and blonde like the foreign women
he'd certainly met some day out in the world.
But he still went out alone. Dressed in white,
his hands behind his back, his face bronzed,
in the mornings he visited fairs and cunningly
bargained for horses. He told me later,
when his plan had failed, that he'd hoped
to buy all the animals in the valley
and force each man to buy a car.
'But I was very stupid,' he said,
'to think I could do so. I should have known
that oxen and people belong together here.'

We walked for more than half an hour. We were close to
    the top,
the wind grew colder, more blustery all the time.
Suddenly my cousin stopped and turned round: 'This year
I'm writing in the manifesto, *Santo Stefano
has always come first in the Belbo valley
celebrations*, and let the people of
Canelli say so.' Then he started up the slope again.
A smell of earth and wind met us out of the darkness,
a few lights in the distance: farms, cars
we could scarcely hear; and I think of the power
which brought this man back to me, snatched him away
    from the sea

back from far-away lands, to the lasting silence.
My cousin didn't speak of the trips he'd made.
He said briefly he'd seen this place or that,
and thought about his cars.

                              Only one dream
remained in his blood: once, working as a stoker
on a Dutch fishing-boat, the *Cetaceo*,
he saw the heavy harpoons flying in the sun,
whales escaping in a froth of blood,
followed them till they reared up and fought them with
    spears.
Sometimes he told me about them.

But when I said that
he was lucky, he had seen dawn
over the loveliest islands in the world,
he smiled at the memory and answered that when the sun
was rising the day was old for them.

(*7–14 September 1930*)

Fallen Women

It's right to treat them like that.
Certainly better than feeling sorry
and then taking them to bed.
'It's the strongest need in all our life' –
but say instead 'We're all condemned to this,
but if ever the girl goes into the trade
I'd choke with rage or take my revenge.'

Pity was always a waste of time,
life is big and pity won't change it,
it's better to grit your teeth in silence.

One evening
I travelled in a train where sat a lady
soberly dressed, made up, a serious look on her face.
Outside, the faint lights and grey-green land
scrubbed out the world. We were alone
in the third-class carriage, the lady and I, who was young.
At that age I didn't know how to talk
and I wept when I thought of women. Like this I made
the journey, nervously on the watch, and she
looked at me sometimes and smoked. I didn't speak,
I certainly didn't think, but still in my blood I feel
that direct gaze, the moment's laughter of someone
who'd worked hard and taken life
as it came, in silence.

A friend, one of those
who has something to say, would like to save
a woman and dry her tears and make her happy.

'No, it's the strongest need in all our life
and if a hard heart is our only strength
and does no good, we're damned.'

You could save thousands of women, but all those
I've seen smoking, with a proud look or a tired smile –
good friends of mine – will always be there
to suffer in silence and pay for everyone.

(*November 1931*)

Ancestors

When the world left me in a daze,
I gave up and moaned to myself.
No fun in hearing men and women
talk if you can't respond.
But even that passed: I'm no longer alone,
I can't respond, but at least I know.
I found companions when I found myself.

I learnt I'd always lived, before I was born,
among men who felt safe and ran their own lives.
Two relatives opened a shop – the first money
in our family; the outsider was earnest,
calculating, ruthless and mean, like a woman.
The other, who was one of us, read novels in his shop –
this mattered in the district – and customers coming in
were briefly told that all the sugar
and even the sulphate had gone. This man, it turned out,
helped the bankrupt brother-in-law.
I felt stronger, thinking of these people,
than when I stood bracing my shoulders in front of the
    mirror
and set my lips in a solemn smile.
One of my forbears, a long time back,
was cheated by a peasant,
then went and tended the vines himself, in summer,
to see the job well done. This is the way
I've always lived, always showing
a brave face and paying in cash.
And women don't count in our family.
I mean, our women stay at home

and bring us into the world and say nothing,
count for nothing, we don't remember them.
Each woman brings us new blood
but effaces herself in the process,
we're the only ones to survive.
We men, we fathers, are full of vices, twitches
and horrors. Someone killed himself,
but one shame has never befallen us:
we'll never be women, never be shadows to others.

I found land when I found companions,
poor land, where it's a privilege
to do nothing and think about the future.
For work alone won't do for me and mine;
we can't uproot ourselves, but our dream
was always honest idleness.
We were born to wander round these hills,
without women, our hands behind our backs.

(*February 1932*)

When I Was a Boy

I don't know why I was there that evening in the fields.
Perhaps I'd flopped down exhausted from the sun
and played the wounded Indian. In those days I
climbed the hills alone, looking for bison,
shot painted arrows and brandished a spear.
That evening I was all tattooed in war-paint.
The air was cool, the lucerne
like deep velvet, sprinkled with reddish-grey
flowers, and the clouds and sky
came half-way up the stalks. The boy lay on his back and
gazed at the sky, he'd heard it praised at the villa.
But the sunset was dazzling. Better to close his eyes,
enjoy the embrace of the grass. It swirled round like
    water.

A sudden hoarse voice reached me out of the sun:
the owner of the field, who didn't like us,
stopping to look at the pool where I lay submerged,
knew me, the boy from the villa, told me in anger
I'd spoil my clothes and had better wash my face.
I jumped half out of the grass. But I stayed there
looking in fear at that darkened face.

A fine chance to shoot a man with an arrow!
The boy wasn't brave enough. I told myself
the man's air of command had stopped me.
Even now I pretend to act with impassive calm,
but I left that night in silence, clutching my arrows,
muttering, shouting out words like a dying hero.
Humiliation perhaps beneath the angry gaze

of someone who could have struck me. I think I was
   ashamed,
like someone who laughs when he hears a coarse joke.
But I fear I was afraid. I had to flee: I fled.
And at night I cried, biting the pillow,
bringing a taste of blood to my mouth.

The man is dead. The lucerne has been harrowed up,
but I see myself vividly in that field,
I feel curious, I walk along and talk to myself, impassive,
like the tall, sunburnt man who spoke to me that evening.

(*15–16 July 1932*)

Encounter

Those hard hills that made my body
and rack it with so many memories, gave me the wonder
of that girl who doesn't know I create but do not under-
   stand her.

I met her one evening: a lighter figure
beneath the ambiguous stars, in the mist of summer.
Round about was the murmur of these hills,
deeper than the shade, and all at once was a sound
that seemed to come from the hills, a voice both clear
and harsh, a voice from times that are lost.

Sometimes I see her, and she lives before me,
clear-cut, immutable, like a memory.
I've never been able to grasp her; her reality
always eludes me, takes me far away.
I don't know if she's beautiful. Among women, she's
   young.
The thought of her recalls a distant memory
of childhood lived among these hills,
she's so young. She's like the morning. All the distant skies
of those far-off mornings beckon to me in her eyes,
those eyes express a clearer light
than dawn has ever revealed over these hills.

I made her from the depth of all the things
that are dearest to me, she's something I don't understand.

(*8–15 August 1932*)

The Paper-Smokers

He took me to hear his band. He sat in a corner
and picked up his trumpet. An infernal racket began.
Outside a raging wind and the rain pelting down between
the lightning seemed to blow the lights out
every five minutes or so. In the darkness the faces
were twisted sideways, playing a dance tune
from memory. My poor friend led them all
from the back of the room. And the trumpet writhed,
broke through the sonorous din, went back and forth
like a lonely soul in a dry silence.

These poor instruments are often mauled about:
these are peasant's hands that touch the keys
and the stubborn foreheads are barely raised from the
    ground.
Wretched and weary blood, worn out
from too much work, can be heard roaring
in the notes, and my friend guides them carefully,
he whose hands are hardened from wielding a hammer
and pushing a plane, wresting a life for himself.

Once he had friends, and he's only thirty.
He belongs to the post-war years, he grew up hungry.
He too came to Turin, seeking a living,
and found injustice. He learnt to work
in the factories, unsmiling. He learnt to measure
the hunger of others against his own fatigue,
and found injustice everywhere. He tried to find peace
by walking half-asleep along the interminable streets
at night, but thousands of brilliant lights
showed only their iniquity: husky-voiced women, drunks,

scattered and staggering puppets. He came to Turin
one winter, among factory glare and slag and smoke;
and he knew what work was. He accepted work
as the harsh destiny of man. But all men
should accept it and there would be justice in the world.
But he made friends. There was endless talk
and he had to listen, waiting for the end.
If they were friends. Every house had families of them.
All round the city there were friends. And the face of the
     world
was covered with them. They felt within themselves
such a desperate need to conquer the world.

They sound harsh tonight, in spite of the band
whom he taught one by one. The rain and the light
don't affect the din. His stern and concentrated face
awaits grief, as he chews his trumpet.
I saw this look in his eyes one evening as we sat alone
with his brother, ten years sadder than him.
We sat by a failing light. His brother was working
at a useless lathe he had built himself.
And my poor friend accused destiny
which kept him tied to the plane and hammer
in order to feed two old unwanted people.

All at once he cried out
that it wasn't destiny if the world suffered,
if the sunlight wrung out curses:
it was men who were guilty. *At least they could go away,
be hungry if they wanted, and say no
to a life that uses love and pity,
the family, the little plot of land, to hold people together.*

(*31 August–11 September 1932*)

Idleness

All the big manifestoes on the walls
show strong workers reaching for the sky
against a factory background –
but they're rotting away in the sun and rain. Masino curses,
seeing his face look proudly down from the walls
while he must tramp the streets and look for work.
He gets up in the morning and stops to look at the
    papers,
at kiosks bright with women's faces in colour:
he meets the ones who pass, and wastes his time.
Each woman has eyes more tired than the last. All at once
the old men dressed in red appear
with cinema posters behind their backs,
walking with measured steps. Masino stares at the
shapeless faces and colours, taps his cheeks and finds them
    more hollow still.

Whenever he eats, Masino starts his rounds again,
it's a sign he's already been working. He crosses the streets,
no longer looks anyone in the face. In the evening he
    returns,
lies briefly in the fields with a girl.
When he's alone he likes to stay in the fields
among the lonely houses and muffled sounds,
and sometimes he sleeps. No shortage of women,
like the time he was still a mechanic: now he wants
one girl only and wants her faithful too.
Once, when going on his rounds, he knocked down a
    rival –
his friends found him in a ditch

and had to bandage his hand. They're out of work now
 as well,
and three or four, because they were hungry, made up a
 band
with a trumpet and guitars; they wanted Masino
to sing and they'd all go round the streets collecting money.
Masino replied that he sang for nothing
whenever he wanted, but trudging
the streets and waking up servant-girls was something
 they did
in Naples. On days when he eats he finds a few friends
and takes them half-way up the hill.
They shut themselves up in an inn and sing a few
solos, all men together. Once they went in a boat,
but they saw the works from the river and it made them
 angry.

After a day spent kicking his heels in front of posters
Masino ended up in the cinema
where he'd worked once before. Darkness comforts
your eyes when they're tired from so many street-lamps.
It isn't hard to follow the story:
you can see pretty girls and sometimes the men
have a really good fight. They are countries
where he could live – never mind
those stupid actors. Against a landscape of fields
and factories and naked hills Masino contemplates
his own head larger than life in the foreground.
At least it doesn't drive him into a rage like the
coloured posters at street-corners and the painted faces of
 women.

(*Winter 1932*)

Deola Thinking

Deola spends the morning in the café
and nobody looks at her. All the city folk
are rushing along in the still-cool sunshine of dawn. Deola
    looks
for no one, but smokes in peace and breathes in the
    morning.
In the *pensione* she had to sleep at this hour
to recover her strength: soldiers and workmen,
clients who wore out her back and marked the mat
by the bed with their dirty shoes. But on your own, it's
    different:
you can work better, you don't get too tired.
The man who came yesterday, waking her suddenly,
kissed her and drove with her (*darling, I'd stay
with you here in Turin, if I could*) to the station
so she could say *bon voyage*.

She's weary but fresh today,
and she likes being free, drinking her milk
and eating brioches. This morning she's half a lady
and looks at the passers-by merely for entertainment.
At this time in the *pensione* they're all asleep, it's stuffy –
the *padrona* has nothing to do – and it's stupid to stay there.
To do the rounds in the evening you need all you've got,
and in the *pensione*, by thirty, you've lost the little you have.

Deola sits profiled against a mirror
and looks at herself in the wall of glass. A little pale about
    the face:
it isn't the smoke in the air. She wrinkles her brow.

With will-power like Marí's she could have stayed
in the *pensione* (*because, dear lady, men*
come here to play games that won't take wives or mistresses
away from them), and Marí worked
untiringly, full of health and vigour.
The passers-by in front of the café don't distract Deola;
she works only in the evening with slow conquests
to the sound of music. Making eyes
at a client or touching his foot, she likes the orchestras
which turn her into an actress playing a love-scene
with a rich young man. One client an evening
is enough, like that she can live. (*Perhaps the man who*
came yesterday will really take me away with him.) To be alone,
    if she wants,
in the morning, and sit in the café looking for no one.

(*5–12 November 1932*)

Landscape I

To Pollo

The hill up there's not cultivated now. Only ferns
and bare rock and sterility.
Work's no use there any longer. The summit's scorched
and your breath's the only coolness. It's hard work
climbing up there: the hermit went up once
and stayed ever since to regain his strength.
The hermit wears goatskins, has
a musky smell of animals and pipe-smoke
which penetrates the ground, the bushes and the grotto.
If he smokes his pipe in the shade
I'll never find him again, for his colour's
the same as the scorched ferns. Visitors climb up,
flop down on a rock, sweating and tired,
and find him stretched out, with his eyes raised to heaven,
breathing deeply. He has achieved one thing:
let his sparse red beard grow on his sun-blackened face.
And he leaves excrement out in the open, to dry in the sun.

The hill slopes and valleys are green and deep.
Along the pathways through the vines go wild groups
of girls in bright-coloured clothes,
to have fun with the goat and shout down to the plain.
Sometimes baskets of fruit appear,
but don't reach the top: the peasants carry them home
on their backs, bent double, and sink down among the
   leaves.
They have too much to do and don't visit the hermit,
but climb up and down, working away.
When they're thirsty, they gulp down wine: with the
   bottle

to their lips, they raise their eyes to the scorched summit.
In the cool morning they go back, worn out already
with the work at dawn, and, if a beggar passes by,
all the water that the wells pour out in harvest-time
is there for the taking. They snigger at groups of ladies
and ask when they'll dress in goatskins,
sit on those hills and go brown in the sun.

(1933)

Away from Home

Too much sea. We have seen enough sea.
Late in the day, when the wide water fades
into wan emptiness, my friend stares at the sea,
I stare at my friend, and we do not speak.
When darkness comes, we shut ourselves away at last, and,
isolated in some smoky room, we drink. My friend has
  his dreams
(somewhat monotonous, dreams to the roar of the tide)
where sea, between one island and another, mirrors only
hills with patterns of wild flowers and waterfalls.
That is the way he drinks. As he looks at his glass
he watches green hills rise from the plain of the sea.
I like hills; and I let him speak of the sea,
for its water is clear and sometimes exposes the rocks.

I see only hills and they fill my earth and sky
with solid shapes that are distant or near.
Only mine are rugged, the ashen soil streaked over
with weary vines. My friend accepts them,
wants to clothe my hills with wild-growing fruit and
  flowers
and gaily discover girls more naked than fruit.
No need: for my harsher dreams are not without laughter.
Tomorrow, if we set out early towards
those hills, we may meet among the vines
some dark girl, her skin black with sunburn,
we may start to talk, and eat some of her grapes.

(1933)

Street Song

Why be ashamed? When you've done your time
and they let you out, you're like everyone else
around the streets who's been inside.

From morning to evening we go round the streets –
come rain or shine, it's always fine for us.
It's great in the street meeting people who talk,
and to chat with them and pick up girls.
It's great to whistle in doorways waiting for girls
and stroll arm-in-arm with them down to the cinema,
and smoke in secret, leaning against their lovely knees.
It's great to talk, to feel them and laugh,
and at night two arms are there to pull you
down in bed; it's great to think of the day
when you come out of prison and the sunshine's cool.

Going round drunk from morning to night
and laughing at everyone passing by, who all
enjoy being out in the streets, even those who are dumb.
Singing drunk from morning to evening
and meeting drunks and starting the talk
which goes on for ever and makes you thirsty.
All these people who go round talking together,
we want them with us at night, shut in the depths of the bar,
we want them following our guitar
which jumps about drunk and won't stay inside any more
but bursts through the doors and echoes through the
    air –
outside there's a rain of water or stars. We don't even care if
the streets are empty of beautiful girls:

we'll find some drunk who's laughing all alone,
he came out of prison tonight as well,
and shouting and singing with him, we'll make the
   morning.

(*1933*)

Landowners

My priest, who was country born, watched over
the dying in the city, night and day, and after so many
  years
collected a little money to leave to the hospital.
He spared only fallen women and children,
and in the new hospital – with its white-painted iron beds –
there's a whole wing for women and waifs.
But the dying who were spared still seek him out
for advice on business. He has grown thin from care,
from moving between sick-beds and ramblings of the
  dying,
from following the dead to their graves whenever he
  could,
praying for them, sprinkling holy water and blessing
  them.

One afternoon in March, in weather already warm, my
  priest
buried an old woman covered with sores: she was his
  mother.
The little lady died at home, for she was afraid
of hospital and wished to die in her own bed.
That day my priest wore the robes he always wore
at burials, but over the coffin
he sprinkled much holy water and prayed even longer.
In the warm afternoon came the smell of the fresh-dug
  earth
over the coffin with its withering corpse: the old woman
died from grief at seeing her land dwindling away;
she was left alone and it was her duty to save it.

Beneath the soil a rosary was twined about the wounded
    hands
which during her life had grown so wretched,
signing three or four papers with a cross. And my priest
    prayed
that this boldness would be forgiven,
of a widow who, while her son studied with priests,
had taken on so much and never sought advice.
The hospital has a garden smelling of earth,
laid out so carefully, providing fresh air for the sick.
My priest knows the trees and bushes
better than his dead, who are ever changing,
while the trees and bushes are always the same.
He mumbles among this greenness – as he does over
    graves –
in moments stolen from the sick, and always forgets
to stop by the grotto which the nuns have made,
showing the Nativity, in the shaded walk. Sometimes he
    complains
that work has always stopped him from keeping an eye
on the dried-up trees, and not once in thirty years
has he found time to think of the eternal requiem.

(*12–16 February 1933*)

A Mania for Solitude

As I eat supper by the light window, it's dark already
inside the room, the sky is darkening too.
Outside, the quiet roads lead
quickly into open country.
I eat and look at the sky – who knows how many women
are eating at this moment – my body is calm;
work stuns my body, it stuns all women.

Outside, after supper, the stars will touch
the wide plain of the earth. The stars are alive,
but not as fine as the cherries I'm eating alone.
I can see the sky, but I know that lights already shine
between the rusty roofs, and sounds are heard beneath
    them.
A deep breath and my body savours the life
of trees and rivers, and feels cut off from everything.
A short silence will do, then everything stops
where it belongs, as my body has stopped.

Everything isolated before my senses,
they accept it without question: a rustle of silence.
I can fathom everything in the darkness
as well as I know the blood in my veins.
The plain is a great rush of water among the grass,
a supper of everything. Each tree, each stone,
lives motionless. I hear my food feeding the veins
of every living thing on this plain.

The night does not matter. The square of sky
whispers all the noises to me, and a tiny star

struggles in the void, far from food,
from houses, different. It's incomplete on its own,
needs too much company. Here in the dark, alone,
my body's at peace and feels itself master.

(27–29 May 1933)

Hard Work (1)

Lying on the grass, fully dressed, they look at each other
between the slender stalks: the woman chews his hair,
then chews the grass. She looks untidy, smiling through
   the grass.
The man seizes the slender hand and bites it
and leans against her body. The woman rolls away from
   him.
Half the grass in the field has been ruffled now.
The girl sits up and tidies her hair
and doesn't look at the man who lies there, open-eyed.

Seated at a table in the evening, they look
at each other, people pass by incessantly.
Now and then some bright colour distracts them.
Now and then he thinks of this useless day off,
spent following this woman
who likes being near him and looking into his eyes.
If he touches her leg with his foot he knows
they'll exchange a look of surprise
and a smile, and the woman's glad. Other women passing
don't look him in the face, but at least they'll undress
with a man tonight. Or perhaps every woman
loves only the man who succeeds in getting nowhere.

All day they've chased each other, the woman's cheeks are
still red from the sun. In her heart she's grateful to him.
She remembers a wild kiss exchanged in a wood,
disturbed by the sound of steps, and it burns her still.
She clasps the green bunch of maidenhair fern
gathered from the rock in a grotto, turns towards him

with a longing glance. He looks at the knot
of blackish stalks through the quivering green,
conscious of desire, of another knot
he can feel below in the light-coloured suit
that the woman knows nothing about. Not even anger
succeeds, for the girl, who loves him, reduces
attacks to a kiss and takes his hands in hers.

But tonight, when he's left her, he knows where he'll go:
he'll get back home flat and worn out,
but at least his satisfied body will relish
the sweetness of sleep in the empty bed.
Only, this is the rub, he'll imagine
the woman's body he'll have as his own,
unashamed and full of desire, will be hers.

(*18–19 July 1933*)

People Who Don't Understand

The lights come on beneath the station trees.
Gella knows her mother's back from the fields
with an apron full of hay. Gella, waiting for the train,
looks into the greenness and smiles at the thought
that she too might stop and gather hay between the lights.

Gella knows her mother was in the city once
when young: she herself leaves every evening when it's
   dark
and on the train remembers reflections in windows
and people who pass and don't look her in the face.
Her mother's town is a courtyard enclosed
by walls, with people leaning on the balcony.
Gella returns each evening, her eyes distracted
by colours and desires, and as she looks from the train
she thinks, to the monotonous rhythm, of clear-cut streets
between lights, of hills crossed by roads, of life
and gaiety of youth, of the freedom of walking and hearing
   the boss's jokes.

Gella's tired of coming and going, of returning at night
and living neither among houses nor vineyards.
She would like the city to be on these hills,
luminous, secret, and never moving again.
It's too scattered the way it is. In the evening she meets
her brothers again, coming back barefoot from work,
her mother looks sunburnt, the talk is of land,
and she sits silent. But she remembers still
when she was a child she too came home with her bundle
   of hay:

only that was a game. And her mother, sweating
as she gathers hay, because she's gathered it
every evening for thirty years, could really for once
stay at home. Nobody wants her.

And Gella would like to stay alone in the fields,
but find the most solitary, go even into the woods.
Stay there until evening, getting dirty in the grass
and even in the mud, and never go back to the city.
Do nothing, for nothing's any use to anyone else.
Like the goats, she'd pull off only the greenest leaves
and fill her hair, burnt and sweaty,
with the night-time dew. Harden her flesh
and blacken it and pull off her clothes, as if they
didn't want her any more in the city. Gella's tired of coming
    and going
and smiles at the thought of going into town
looking all untidy and dirty. As long as the hills and the
    vines
are there and she can walk
through the streets, where the fields were, in the evening,
    laughing,
this is what Gella wants, as she looks out from the train.

(*29–31 July 1933*)

Building a House

When the cane-brakes went, so did the shade. The sun
   already shines
obliquely through the arches, spills through the blanks
that will soon be windows. The bricklayers work a little,
as long as morning lasts. Now and then they complain:
when the canes were still growing here
a passer-by who felt too hot could fling himself on the
   grass.

The boys are starting to get closer to the sun.
They're not afraid of the heat. The single pillars against
   the sky
are a better playground than trees
or the familiar street. The bare bricks
are filling with blue as the vaults
are closing, and the boys love seeing from below
the square of sky above their heads. A pity it's fine,
a shower of rain up there on the empty spaces
would please the boys. It would wash the house.

It was certainly better last night – they were able to come:
the dew bathed the bricks and between the walls
they could see the stars. They could even light
a good fire and fight and throw stones.
A stone thrown at night can fall without a sound.
Then there are adders that climb down the walls
and fall like a stone, though more softly.

Something happens at night in there, only
the old man knows, the one who comes down over the
   hills.

He leaves remains of a fire there and his beard is singed
by the blaze, he's already drunk so much water that like
   the ground
he couldn't change colour. He makes everyone laugh,
saying the others are sweating to build the house
while he sleeps there and doesn't sweat at all. But an old
   man
shouldn't last, sleeping at night in the open.
Not like a couple in a field: a man and a woman
who hold each other tight and then go home.
But the old man hasn't a house any more and moves
   wearily.
Certainly something happens to him in there,
for in the morning he's still talking to himself.

Soon the bricklayers lie down in the shade.
The sun's invaded everything now,
and if you touch a brick you burn your hands.
An adder's already been seen rushing
into the pool of lime: the heat now
makes even the beasts impatient. They have a drink
and see the other hills all round, burning hot,
shimmering in the sun. Only a fool
would go on working, and in fact the old man
is crossing the vineyards now, stealing the pumpkins.
Then there are boys on the bridges, climbing up and down.
Once a stone fell on the boss's head
and everyone stopped work for a time
to take him to the stream and wash his face.

(1933)

Those Who Are Not Convinced

The rain falling on the squares and streets,
the barracks and the hill, is all wasted.
Tomorrow morning the trees will be washed,
along the roads, and the barrack-square so soft
we'll splash through the mud: all the work they do in the
   city
resembles this water that falls on the roofs.

   (Outside, it rains in the dark over all the streets,
   by tomorrow the grass will be growing.)

The water came flowing down tonight
along the ditches, on the hill, the soil all yellow
with leaves and mud. But above the smell
of earth a sterile and musty scent of flowers
sucking in water, and among the flowers, the villas
dripping with rain. Only from the other slope
a smell of vines drifts in on the wind.

   (Outside, it rains in the dark on the squares and
      streets,
   but no matter: wine comes to warm us
   with a warmth we'll still feel tomorrow.)

There's a smell of stone washed in the wind,
and on the ground only wheel-tracks. I don't know
any of the women passing. City women
are always different, they aren't any good.
In the brothel things smell good

and the women are fine. But even they live
as though in barracks and the work they do is stupid.

   (No matter: the women will come to warm us
   with a warmth we'll still feel tomorrow.)

(*Summer 1933*)

Nocturnal Pleasures

We too stop to smell the night,
just when the wind is bleakest: the roads
are cold with wind, every smell has faded;
our nostrils are raised to the flickering lights.

We all have a house that waits in the dark
for us to return: a woman awaits us in the dark,
lying asleep: the room is warm with smells.
The woman who sleeps and breathes knows nothing
about the wind, the warmth of her body
the same as the blood that murmurs within us.

This wind washes us, coming from the depths
of the roads lying open in the dark; the flickering
lights and our raised nostrils confront
each other squarely. Every smell is a memory.
From far away in the dark the wind dislodges
whatever lies in the city: down over fields and hills,
where there is only grass scorched by the sun
and soil blackened by damp. Our memory
is a bitter taste, the little sweetness
of the rent earth exhaled in winter
in a breath from below. Every smell has faded
away in the dark and in the city only the wind can reach
    us.

We'll go back tonight to the woman who sleeps,
searching her body with icy fingers,
and heat will shake our blood, the heat of earth

blackened with damp: a breath of life.
She too has been warmed in the sun and now reveals
in her nakedness her sweetest life,
which vanishes by day, and tastes of earth.

(*1933*)

Mediterranean

My friend says little and at random.
Is it worth meeting him one windy morning?
One of us at dawn has left a woman.
We could talk about the damp wind,
the calm or some passer-by, as we watch the street;
but no one begins. My friend's far away,
when he smokes he doesn't think. He's unaware.

                                    The Negro
was smoking too, when we both saw him one morning,
standing in the corner drinking wine –
outside, the sea was waiting. But the redness of the wine
and the lovely cloud were not for him:
he wasn't thinking of the taste. Not even the morning
kept the taste of dawn;
a monotonous day, detached from time
for the Negro. The image of a distant country
lent him background. But he didn't belong.

There were women about and the light was fresher,
and the smell of the sea ran through the streets.
We didn't want either the women or the walk: just
to sit there and listen to life and think that the sea
was there, beneath the sun still fresh from sleep.
White women passed, our women, before the Negro
who didn't even look down at his hands
that were too dark, didn't even catch his breath.
We had left a woman, and everything
in the dawn knew of our possessing:
the calm, the street, and the wine.

This time passers-by
distract me and then I forget my friend
who began to smoke in the damp wind
but doesn't seem to be happy.

Soon afterwards he asked me:
Do you remember that Negro who was smoking and
drinking?

(*1934*)

Green Wood

To Massimo Mila

There are hills in front of him as he stands in the dark.
As long as these hills consist of earth
the peasants will have to dig them. He looks and does not
    see them,
like the man who shuts his eyes in prison, wide-awake.
The man standing there – who's been in prison – starts work
again tomorrow with a few friends. Tonight he's alone.

He smells rain on the hills; the distant smell
that sometimes reached the prison on the wind.
Sometimes it rained in the city: refreshing
breath and blood in the wide, open street.
The prison took the rain, in prison life
did not end, but sometimes the sun filtered through:
his friends waited and the future waited.

Now he's alone. The silent smell of the earth
seems to come from his own body, and distant memories –
he knows the land – bind him to the soil,
the real soil. No point in thinking
the peasants strike the soil with their spades
as they strike an enemy, and hate each other with
murderous hate. But they have
one joy: this piece of cultivated land.
What do others matter? Tomorrow in the sun
the hills will be there, each man has his own.

His friends don't live in the hills,
they were born in the city where instead of grass
there are tram-lines. Sometimes even he forgets.

But the smell of earth which reaches the city
knows nothing of peasants any more. It's a long caress
which makes you close your eyes and think of your friends
in prison, of the long-lasting prison that waits.

(1934)

A Generation

A boy would come to play in the fields
where now there are streets. He found in the fields
other boys, barefooted too, and he'd jump for joy.
It was fun to take off his shoes in the grass with them.
One evening of distant lights they would hear echoes of
    shots
in the city, and on the wind came frightened
and broken shouting. Everyone was silent.
On the hillsides gleams
of light flared up in the wind. The night would grow
dark, in the end extinguishing everything,
and during sleep came only cool puffs of wind.

(Next morning the boys go back to play
and no one remembers the noise. There are
workers in prison, silent, and someone's already dead.
They've covered up the blood-stains in the streets.
In the distance the city wakes in the sun
and people go out. They look each other in the face.)
The boys would think of the darkness in the fields
and stare at the women. Even the women
would say nothing and let things be.
The boys thought of the darkness in the fields
where a girl would come. It was fun making girls
cry in the dark. We were those boys.
We liked the town by day: at night we were silent
and looked at the distant lights and listened to the noise.

Boys still go to play in the fields
at the end of the streets. And night is the same.

As we walk by we can smell the grass.
The same people are in prison. And the women are
still there, they have babies and say nothing.

(1934)

Afterwards

Silent rain covers the hill.

It rains over the houses: the low window
has filled with a fresher, barer green.
She lay beside me: the window
was blank, saw nothing, we were naked.
At this hour the body goes through the street in secret
with the same step, but the rhythm is softer; the rain
falls like that footstep, light and weary.
She doesn't see the bare hill
sleeping in the dampness: she walks through the street
and the people she meets do not know.

Evening comes,
a few flakes of snow fall on the hill,
the window feels their breath. The street
at this time is deserted: the hill
has a distant life in its darker body.
We lay weary in the dampness
of two bodies sleeping together.

On a warmer evening, with tepid sun
and brighter colours, the street would be a delight.
A delight to go down the street, enjoying
the memory of a body all diffused within.

In the leaves along the avenue, in the indolent walk of
      women,
in everyone's voice there is something of the life
that the two bodies have forgotten, but a miracle no less.

Discovering the hill at the end of a street,
between the houses, looking and thinking that
she can see it too from the little window.

The bare hill has melted into the dark
and the rain whispers. She's not here,
she has gone with her soft body and her smile.
But tomorrow beneath the dawn-washed sky
she'll go out with her light step
into the streets. We'll meet, if we feel so inclined.

(1934)

Revolt

The dead man's distorted, doesn't look at the stars:
his hair's stuck to the pavement. It's colder at night.
The living go back home, shuddering.
It's hard to go with them; they're all shocked,
some climb steps and some go down into dives.
One goes on until dawn and collapses
in a sunlit field. Tomorrow someone sobs
in desperation, at work. Then even that passes.

When they sleep, they seem dead: if there's a woman too
the smell's stronger, but they look dead.
Each body lies distorted on its bed
as on the red pavement: the long weariness
till dawn equals a brief agony.
Dark sweat congeals on every body.
But that dead man lies out in the open.

The heap of rags that the sun burns against
the wall looks dead too. Sleeping
on the pavement shows faith in the world.
There's a beard among the rags and busy flies crawl
over it; passers-by move along the street
like flies, the beggar's part of the street.
Poverty covers his leering face with a beard
like grass and gives an air of peace. This old man
who could die distorted, bloody,
seems instead an object, he's alive. Like this,
save for the blood, every object is part of the street.
But in the street the stars have seen blood.

(1934)

Sad Supper

Supper beneath the pergola,
water running quietly below.
We sit in silence watching and listening to the sound
of the water in the moonlight.
This lingering is delightful.

                    My companion dawdles,
she might still be eating that bunch of grapes,
her mouth's so bright; and the taste lingers
like the yellow moonlight in the air. Her glance, in the
    dusk,
is as sweet as the grapes, but her strong shoulders
and sunburnt cheeks contain the whole of summer.

Grapes and bread left on the white table.
The two deserted chairs face each other.
Who knows what the moonlight reveals,
with its gentle light, in the distant woods.
Then at dawn a colder breeze
can blow away moon and mist, and someone appears.
A faint light shows the gulping
throat and the fevered hands vainly
grabbing at the food. The water goes on running,
but in the dark. Neither grapes nor bread have moved.
Flavours torment the famished wraith
who can't even lick from the grapes
the dew that's already on them. Glittering
in the dawn, the chairs face each other, alone.
Sometimes down by the water there's a smell
like grapes, a stagnant female smell on the grass,

and the moon shines in silence. Someone appears,
yet comes through the trees like a ghost, moans
hoarsely like a voiceless creature,
lies down on the grass and doesn't touch the soil:
only the nostrils quiver. It's cold at dawn,
and the embrace of a body would be life.
Stronger than the yellow moonlight, which has a horror
of filtering into the woods, is this endless yearning
for touch and taste that consumes the dead.
At other times rain on the soil torments them.

(*1934*)

Portrait of the Author

To Leone Ginzburg

The window looking down on to the pavement
is always blank. The blue of summer overhead
seems more stable, yet a cloud comes up.
Nobody comes here. And we're sitting on the ground.

My friend – how he stinks – sitting with me
in the public street, has pulled his trousers off
without moving his body. I take off my pullover.
It's cold on the stone and my friend enjoys it
more than I who watch him, but nobody passes.
Suddenly the window reveals a woman,
pale in colour. She's certainly smelt that smell
and looks at us. My friend's already standing up to look.
He's got hair all the way from his face to his legs –
he doesn't need trousers – and the hair bursts through
the holes in his pullover. It's self-sufficient hair.
My companion has jumped through that window
into the dark, and the woman has gone. My eyes move
to the strip of solid sky, which is also naked.

I don't stink, for I'm not hairy. The stone freezes me,
my bare back which women like
because it's smooth: what don't they like?
But no women pass. Instead a bitch passes,
followed by a dog that stinks
from the rain. The smooth cloud in the sky
remains motionless: it looks like a mass of leaves.
My friend's found supper this time.
Women treat men well when they're naked. At last
a boy comes round the corner, smoking.

He's got legs like a snake as well, curly hair,
hard skin: one fine day the women will want to undress
   him
and sniff out whether he stinks.
When he comes up I stick my foot out. He falls down
   quickly
and I ask him for a stub. We smoke in silence.

(*1934*)

Hard Work (2)

Only a boy crosses the street to run away
from home, but the man going round
the streets all day isn't a boy any more
and he's not running away from home.

            In summer there are
afternoons with empty squares lying
beneath the hot sun, and this man, reaching
an avenue of useless trees, stops.
Is it worth being alone if you get lonelier still?
When you just go round the squares and streets,
they're empty. He wants to stop a woman
and talk to her and persuade her they'll live together.
Otherwise you talk to yourself. And that's why sometimes
at night a drunk starts
telling you the whole long story of his life.

Waiting in the empty square there's no guarantee
he'll meet someone, but anyone trudging the streets
stops a while sometimes. If there were two of them,
both going round the streets, home would be
wherever the woman was, it would be worth it.
At night the square is deserted again
and the man passing doesn't see the houses
between the useless lights, he doesn't look up any more;
he feels only the pavement, which other men have made
with hardened hands like his.
No point in staying in the deserted square.
There'll certainly be some woman in the street
who'll take him home with her if he asks her.

(1934)

Motherhood

This man has had three sons: a big heavy
body, sufficient unto itself; watching him pass,
you imagine his sons must have the same build.
Three young men resembling him must have sprung
ready-made from the father's limbs,
the woman doesn't count. But despite the three bodies,
there's no part missing from
the father's limbs: the boys detached themselves
as they walked along beside him.

                 The woman existed,
she had a strong body, gave
her blood to each son and died from the third.
It's strange to the three young men, living without the
    woman
they don't know, who gave her strength to bear them,
eclipsed herself in them. The woman was young
and laughed and talked, but taking part in life
is a risky joke. That was how the woman
went into silence, gazing bewildered at her man.

The three sons shrug their shoulders
in a way the man remembers. None of them
knows that his eyes and body have a life
which in its time was full and satisfied the man.
But watching one of the boys as he leans
over the river and dives, the man no longer feels
the flash of her limbs in the water and the joy
of their bodies submerged. He doesn't see his sons
any more if he meets them face to face in the street.

How long ago were his sons born? The three young men
are arrogant now, one of them's already
got a son by mistake, without getting the woman.

(*1934*)

Grappa in September

The mornings pass clear and empty
by the banks of the river, which at dawn is misted
a darker green, waiting for the sun.
The tobacco they sell in the last house at the edge of the
     fields,
which is still damp, is nearly black,
has a juicy taste: it makes blue smoke.
They have grappa too, the colour of water.

A moment has come when everything stops
and ripens. The trees in the distance are still:
they've grown darker. There's hidden fruit
which would fall if you shook it. The scattered clouds
are round with ripeness. Far away in the streets
each house ripens in the warmth of the sun.

At this time there are only women about. The women
     don't smoke
and don't drink, they only know how to stand in the
     sun
and receive its warmth all over, like fruit.
The air, keen with mist, can be sipped slowly
like grappa, everything has its taste.
Even the river-water has drunk the banks
and soaks them in the sky. The streets
are like women, ripening slowly.

At this time everyone should stop
in the street and watch how everything ripens.

There's even a breeze, which doesn't move the clouds,
but it's strong enough to stir the blue smoke
without breaking it up: it's a new taste which drifts by.
And the tobacco tastes of grappa. Like this the women
aren't the only ones to relish the morning.

(*1934*)

Ulysses

The old man's fed up, his son was born
too late. Sometimes they look each other in the face,
but once is enough for a slap. (The old man goes out,
comes back with his son who pulls a face
and won't raise his eyes any more.) Now the old man sits
until night-time in front of a big window,
but no one comes and the street's deserted.

This morning the boy ran off, and came back
at night. He sits there sobbing. He won't tell
anyone if he's eaten at noon. He'll even
be heavy-eyed and he'll go to bed in silence:
his shoes are muddy. This morning was fine
after a month of rain.

                    Through the cool window
comes a bitter smell of leaves. But the old man
doesn't move from the darkness, hasn't slept all night,
and would like to sleep and forget the whole thing
as though he'd returned from a long walk.
To keep himself warm he yelled once and struck out.

The boy soon came back, his father didn't hit him any
    more.
The boy's a young man now and every day
discovers something and doesn't talk to anyone.

There's nothing in the street he couldn't discover
by standing at the window. But the boy walks

the streets all day. He doesn't go after women yet
and no longer plays outside. He always comes home.
The boy has his own way of leaving the house
and it's plain there's nothing more to be done.

(*1935*)

August Moon

Beyond the yellow hills is the sea,
beyond the clouds. But endless days
and undulating hills that shimmer against the sky
lie in front of the sea. Up there are the olive-trees,
the pool of water too small to mirror your face,
and the stubble, the never-ending stubble.

And the moon rises. Her husband's lying
in a field, his head split open by the sun –
a wife can't drag a corpse along
like a sack. The moon rises, throwing a little shade
beneath the twisted branches. The woman in the shade
glares in terror at the big bloody face
that's congealing and soaking every fold in the hills.
The corpse stretched out in the fields doesn't move,
neither does the woman in the shade. Only the eye full of
    blood
seems to wink at someone and show him the way.

Long shudders of cold come down from the bare distant
hills, and the woman feels them on her shoulders,
as when they rippled across the sea of grain.
The spreading olive-branches also encroach on
this sea of moonlight, already the shade of the tree
seems a narrowing cage that swallows her up as well.

She rushes out, in the moonlit horror,
and the rustling breeze follows her over the stones
and a thin mould which eats into the trees

and the pain in her womb. Bent double she goes back to the
   shade
and throws herself on the stones and bites her lip.
Beneath her the dark earth is bathed in blood.

(*Brancaleone, August 1935*)

Landscape VI

This is a day when mist rises from the river
into the lovely city, between the fields and hills,
and clouds it over like a memory. The haze blends
all the greens in one, but the women in bright colours
still walk along. They go into the white half-light
smiling: in the street anything can happen.
The air can make you drunk.

               The morning
will lie open in a broad silence
that stills every voice. Even the beggar,
who has no city or house, will breathe it in
as he breathes in the glass of grappa when he hasn't eaten.
It's worth being hungry or being betrayed
by a sweeter taste in the mouth, even going out in this
    weather
and finding happier memories as he breathes.

Every street, every corner showing
through the mist, preserves an old shudder:
he who feels it can't abandon himself. He can't abandon
his calm ecstasy, made up of things
from a richer life, discovered
in a house or an inn, or from a sudden thought.
Even the big horses which have passed
through the mist at dawn will speak of that time.

Or even a boy who ran away from home and
returns just today, when the mist comes up

from the river, forgets the whole of life,
suffering, hunger and faith betrayed,
as he stops at a corner, drinking in the morning.
It's worth coming back, even if he's changed.

(*Brancaleone, September 1935*)

Poggio Reale

A little window on to the quiet sky
soothes the heart; someone died here peacefully.
Outside there are trees and clouds, the earth
and sky too. The murmur floats up here –
the whole din of life.

       The blank window
reveals only hills beneath the trees,
and a river winding clearly in the distance.
The water's as clear as the wind's breath,
but nobody goes bathing there.

       A cloud appears
solid and white, drifting on to the square of sky.
It sees sleeping houses and hills, everything
visible in the air; it sees lost birds
gliding in the air. People walk quietly along
beside the river and no one notices
the little cloud.

       Now the blue sky is blank
through the little window: the sudden squawk
of a bird breaks through the silence. Perhaps that cloud
is touching the trees or coming down into the river.
The man lying in the field must feel it
in the breath of the grass. But his gaze doesn't move,
only the grass moves. He must be dead.

(*Brancaleone, 15 September 1935*)

The Political Prisoner

We went early to the fishmarket
for a change of scene: silver,
scarlet, green, colour of the sea.
The sea was all silver-scaled,
the fish were brighter. We thought about going home.

The women too were lovely, with amphora on their heads,
olive-green, shaped smooth and rounded
like their hips: we all thought about the women,
how they talk, laugh and walk in the street.
We all laughed. It rained over the sea.

The water soaks the leaves, the last grapes on
the vines hidden in the valleys. The sky's
coloured with scattered clouds, rosy
with gaiety and sun. Savour on the ground
and colour in the sky. Nobody with us.

We thought about going home, like thinking
in the morning after a sleepless night.
We relished the moist fruit,
the bright fish, so alive in the dank sea.
We were drunk, we were going home soon.

(*Brancaleone, September 1935*)

Myth

One day the young god will be a man,
without pain, with the wan smile of the man
who has understood. The distant sun still
shines red on the beaches. The day will come when the god
no longer knows where lay the beaches of the past.

We wake one morning when summer is dead,
before us a tumult still of splendour
like yesterday, and in our ears the crashing of the sun
turned blood. The colour of the world has changed.
The mountain no longer touches the sky; the clouds
no longer hang in masses like fruit; no pebbles
show in the water. The body of a thoughtful man
stands bowed, where once there breathed a god.

The great sun is over, and the smell of earth,
and the open street, coloured with people
unaware of death. One doesn't die in summer.
If someone vanished, it was the young god
who lived for all and knew no death.
Sorrow was the shadow of a cloud above him.
His footsteps astonished the earth.

        Now tiredness
weighs upon all the man's limbs,
without pain: the calm tiredness of dawn
starting a day of rain. The darkened beaches
do not know the young man, when once a glance
was enough. Nor does the sea of air revive
at his breath. The man's lips curve
more calmly as they smile at the earth.
(*Brancaleone, October 1935*)

Simplicity

The lonely man – who's been in prison – goes back to
   prison
each time he eats a piece of bread.
In prison he dreamt of hares hiding
in the winter leaves. In the wintry snow
he lives between the walls of the street, drinking
cold water and biting a piece of bread.

You believe that later life returns,
that breathing grows calmer, that winter returns
with the smell of wine in the warm tavern,
a good fire, the stable, and supper. You believe –
until you're inside you believe. They go out one evening
and catch hares, which others eat
gaily in the warmth. You have to watch them through the
   window.

The lonely man dares to go in and have a drink
when it's really freezing, and gazes at his wine:
the smoky colour, the heavy taste.
He eats a piece of bread, he who smelt the hare
in prison, but now he no longer knows what bread is
or anything else. And even the wine tastes of fog.

The lonely man thinks of those fields, glad
to know they're already ploughed. In the empty room
he tries to sing under his breath. He sees again
along the banks the clumps of bare brambles
which in August were green. He whistles to his dog.
And the hare appears, and they don't feel cold any more.

(*Brancaleone, October 1935*)

Alter Ego

From morning till evening he saw the tattoo
on his silky chest: a russet woman,
lying concealed in the field of hair. Beneath there was
sometimes chaos, she leapt up suddenly.
The day passed in cursing and silence.
If the woman were no tattoo but
clung alive to his hairy chest, he'd
cry out more loudly in the little cell.

Wide-eyed, he lay silently stretched on the bed.
A deep sealike sigh swelled
the big solid bones in his body: he lay
as on a boat-deck. He rested heavily on the bed
like someone who on waking might jump up.
His body, salted with spray, poured out
sweat full of sunshine. The little cell
was not big enough for a single one of his glances.
His hands showed he was thinking of the woman.

(*Brancaleone, October 1935*)

Instinct

From the door of his house in the gentle sunshine
the old man, disillusioned with everything,
watches the dog and the bitch as they follow instinct.

Flies crawl round his toothless mouth.
His wife died some time ago. She too
like all bitches didn't want to hear it mentioned,
but she had the instinct. The old man would smell it
   out –
he hadn't yet lost his teeth – night would come,
they'd go to bed. Instinct was fine.

It's fine for dogs having so much freedom,
prowling the streets from dawn to dusk,
eating a little, sleeping a little, mounting bitches a little:
they don't even wait for night. They reason
as they smell and what they smell is good.

The old man remembers how once in the daytime
he had it in a field of wheat.
Who the bitch was he no longer knows, but remembers
the hot sun and the sweat and his wish it would last for
   ever.
It was like being in bed. If the years could return
he'd like to do it always in a field of wheat.

A woman comes down the street and stops to watch;
the priest passes and turns away. In the public square

you can do anything. Even the woman,
too discreet to turn round for a man, stops.
Only a boy can't stand the game
and pelts them with stones. The old man's angry.

(*Brancaleone, November 1935*)

Tolerance

Rain without a sound on the field of the sea.
Through the foul streets, no one passing.
A solitary woman stepped off the train:
beneath her coat her light skirt showed
and her legs vanished through the black doorway.

It might be a country submerged. The evening
creeps coldly under all the doors, the houses
pour out blue smoke in the dark. The windows
blaze dark red. A light burns
between the closed shutters on the black painted house.

Next day is cold, there's sun on the sea.
A woman in a skirt rinses her mouth
at the fountain, and the water is pink. She has coarse
blonde hair, like orange-peel lying
on the ground. Reaching to the fountain she looks askance at
a grubby urchin who watches, fascinated.
Gloomy women open shutters in the square –
their husbands are still dozing in the dark.

When evening returns, the rain begins again,
spluttering on many fires. The wives,
blowing on the coal, eye the black
house and the deserted fountain. The shutters
on the house are closed, but inside is a bed,
where a blonde woman earns her living.
Everyone rests at night,
everyone save the blonde who washes in the morning.

(*Brancaleone, December 1935*)

The Morning Star

The man who lives alone gets up while the sea's still dark
and the stars waver. A warm breeze
rises over the sea and the shore,
softening the air. This is the time when nothing
can happen. Even the pipe between his teeth
hangs empty. He bathes quickly at night.
Already he's lit a big fire of branches
and watches it redden the ground. Even the sea
will soon be blazing like the fire.

There's nothing more bitter than starting a day
when nothing will happen. Nothing more bitter
than uselessness. A greenish star,
surprised by dawn, hangs tired in the sky.
It sees the still-dark sea and the glow of the fire,
where the man warms his hands for the sake of doing
      something;
it looks on and falls asleep between the sombre mountains
with their bed of snow. The slowness of time
is unrelenting for someone who expects nothing.

Is it worth the sun's rising from the sea
and the long day's beginning? Tomorrow
the lukewarm dawn and transparent light will return,
it will be like yesterday and nothing will ever happen.
The man who lives alone would like only to sleep.
When the last star fades from the sky
he slowly fills and lights his pipe.

(*9–12 January 1936*)

Deola's Return

I'll turn round in the street and look at the passers-by,
I'll be a passer-by myself. I'll learn
how to get up and lay aside the horror
of night and go out walking as I used to.
I'll apply my mind to work for a time,
I'll go back there, by the window, smoking
and relaxed. But my eyes will be the same,
my gestures too, and my face. That empty secret
that lingers in my body and dulls my gaze
will die slowly to the rhythm of the blood
where everything vanishes.

                              I'll go out one morning,
I won't have a house any more, I'll go out in the street;
the night's horror will have left me;
I'll be frightened of being alone. But I'll want to be alone.
I'll look at passers-by with the dead smile
of someone who's beaten, but doesn't hate or cry out,
for I know that since ancient times fate –
all that you've been or will ever be – is in the blood,
in the murmur of the blood. I'll wrinkle my brows
alone, in the middle of the street, listening for an echo
in the blood. And there'll be no echo any more,
I'll look up and gaze at the street.

(*March–April 1936*)

Habit

Moonlight a silent lake on the asphalt road
and other times remembered.
A chance encounter was once enough, then
he wasn't alone any more. Watching the moon
he'd breathe the night in. But fresher the scent
of the woman encountered, the brief romance
up the unsteady stairs. The quiet room
and the sudden wish to live there always
filled his heart. Then, in the moonlight,
back he went with weary strides, content.

In those days he was a good friend to himself.
He would wake up in the morning and leap out of bed,
finding his body again and his old thoughts.
He liked going out in rain or shine,
he liked watching the streets,
talking to people casually. He thought
he could always start afresh
and change his job, when morning came.
When really worn out he would sit and smoke.
His greatest pleasure was being alone.

He's grown old, he'd like a house
that meant more to him, he'd like to go out at night
and stop in the road to look at the moon,
but find at home a submissive woman,
a quiet woman waiting patiently.
He's grown old, he's no longer self-sufficient.
The passers-by are still the same; the rain too

and the sun are the same; and the morning, a desert.
There's no point in working. And no point,
when there's nobody waiting, in going out in the
moonlight.

(*August 1936*)

Summer (1)

She's reappeared, the woman with the half-closed eyes
and firm body, walking along the street.
She held out her hand, her gaze was direct
in the silent street. Everything came back.

In the motionless light of distant day
memory sickened. The woman raised
her artless brow and her old look
returned. Hand outstretched to hand
and tense anxiety the same as before.
All things regain their colours and life
from her distant gaze, her half-closed mouth.

Again the anxiety of distant days,
when a whole summer, motionless, unforeseen
in colour and warmth emerged, with the gaze
of those submissive eyes. Anxiety has returned.
No sweetness of parted lips
can lessen it. A motionless sky waits
coldly, in those eyes.

                    Memory was calm
in the submissive light of time, dying quietly
as the window clouded over and disappeared.
Memory sickened. The tense anxiety
in her light touch has rekindled the colours
of summer and warmth beneath the vivid sky.
But the half-closed mouth and the submissive glances
bring only hard inhuman silence.

(7–9 October 1937)

Friend Sleeping

What shall we say tonight to the friend sleeping?
The slightest word leaps to our lips
from deepest pain. We'll look at our friend,
his useless lips that say nothing,
we'll speak submissively.

     Night will resemble
the old grief each dusk returning,
impassive and alive. Remote silence
will suffer like a soul, mute, in the darkness.
We shall speak to the night which breathes submissively.

We shall hear the moments flow in the darkness
beyond things, in the anxiety of dawn
which will come suddenly, revealing objects
against the silence of death. Useless light
will lay bare the absorbed face of day. Moments
will be silent. And objects will speak submissively.

(*20 October 1937*)

Indifference

This hate has blossomed like a living love,
grieving, watching its own exhaustion.
It seeks a face, it seeks flesh, as though it were love.

The worldly flesh and the voices that spoke
are dead, all has shuddered away,
all life hangs on a voice.
Days pass in bitter ecstasy to the sad
caress of the voice that returns
and drains the blood from our faces. Not without sweetness
that voice returns to the mind exhausted
and trembling: once it trembled for me.

But the flesh does not tremble. Only love
could set it alight, this hate seeks it out.
All the possessions, all the flesh and all the voices
in the world cannot equal the burning caress
of that body and those eyes. In the bitter ecstasy
that kills itself, this hate still finds
each day a glance, a broken word,
and grasps them, hungrily, like love.

(*24 October 1937*)

Jealousy

The old man has the land by day, and by night
a woman of his own – she was his till yesterday.
Taking her pleased him like laying bare the earth,
he would gaze at her lying in the dark
and waiting. She'd smile with her eyes closed.

Tonight the old man sits by the edge
of his field, but doesn't fence or stretch out his hand
to pull up a weed. Between the furrows he turns
over a stray thought. The earth shows
when someone has touched it and broken it up,
shows it even in the dark. But no living woman
retains the shadow of a man's embrace.
The old man knows the woman only smiles
with closed eyes, waiting, lying on her back,
and knows all at once that over the youthful body
moves the embrace of another memory.
The old man can't see the field any more in the dark.
He goes down on his knees, grasping the earth
as though it were a woman and knew how to speak.
But the woman who lies in the dark doesn't speak.

The woman lying with closed eyes in the dark neither
    speaks
nor smiles tonight, from her tight mouth
to her pale shoulder. Her body shows
at last the embrace of a man: the only one
that could mark her, and took her smile away.

(*2–3 November 1937*)

The Country Whore

The front wall of the yard
often reflects the early sun
as the cowshed did. And the untidy room,
deserted in the morning when she wakes,
smells of the first, ingenuous perfume.
Even the body beneath the sheet is the same
as it was before, when her heart leapt in discovery.

Memories come when she wakes alone early
in the morning, and in the dark twilight returns
the ease of that other awakening: the cowshed
of childhood days, exhaustion from the hot
sun when she walked out slowly. A light
scent added to the customary sweat
of her hair, and the animals snuffling. Furtively
her body enjoyed the sun's caress,
insinuating, calm, as though it had touched her.

Getting out of bed deadens her limbs,
still young and stocky like a child's.
The innocent girl would search out the smell
of tobacco and hay and tremble at the fleeting
touch of a man: she liked playing.
Sometimes she would play lying down with the man
in the hay, but the man didn't smell her hair,
he searched in the hay for her tense limbs,
wearing them out, squeezing them as though he were her
    father.
The perfume was that of flowers crushed under stones.
Often as she wakes up slowly she smells again

that liquid smell of long-lost flowers,
cowshed and sun. No man would know
the subtle caress of that bitter memory.
No man sees beyond the body lying there
that tense and awkward childhood.

(*11–15 November 1937*)

The Drunken Old Woman

The old woman likes lying on the ground
and spreading out her arms. The heavy heat
crushes her little face as it crushes the earth.
When things burn, only the soil remains.
Men and wine have betrayed and consumed these bones,
taut brown in their clothes, but the split earth
roars like a flame. There is no word,
there is no regret. The vibrant day returns
when this body too was young, more burning hot than
   the sun.

In memory the great hills return,
alive and young as this body, and the man's look
and the bitterness of the wine revive her tense
desire: heat flared in the blood
like greenness in the grass. Among vines and pathways
memory becomes reality. The old woman, eyes closed
and motionless, enjoys the sky with the body that once
   was hers.

In the split earth there beats a healthier heart
like the strong chest of a father or a man.
She sucks in her wrinkled cheek. Even her father,
even her husband, died betrayed. Even
in them the flesh was consumed. Neither the heat
of their flanks nor the sharpness of wine ever rouses them
   now.

Among the spreading vines the voice of sunlight
murmurs in the transparent fire,

as the air quivers. The grass quivers around her.
The grass is as young as the heat of the sun.
The dead are young in her live memory.

(*22–28 November 1937*)

The Boatman's Wife

Sometimes in the warm sleep of dawn,
dreaming alone, she thinks she's married a woman.

A woman detached from the motherly body,
she's thin and white and lowers her little head
in the room. In the cold, glimmering light she
doesn't wait for morning; she works away. It happens
in silence: there are no words between women.

While she sleeps, the wife knows the boat's on the river,
with rain steaming off the man's back.
But the little wife closes the door quickly
and leans against it and raises her eyes to the other's.
A shower of rain drums noisily on the window,
and the woman lying down, who chews slowly,
holds out a plate. The little wife fills it
and sits on the bed and starts to eat.

The little wife eats quickly, furtively,
beneath the maternal gaze, as though she were a child,
and pushes aside the hand reaching out for her neck.
Suddenly she runs to the door and opens it: the boats
are all tied up alongside. She comes back
barefoot to the bed and they embrace quickly.

The lips she encounters are cold and thin,
but the body melts with a deep and tormenting
heat. Then the little wife sleeps
lying against the mother's body. She's as slender
and sharp as a boy, but she sleeps like a woman.
She wouldn't know how to sail a boat in the rain.

Outside, the rain comes down in the dim light
of the half-open door. A breath of wind enters
the empty room. If the door opened
the man would come in, the man who's seen everything.
He wouldn't say a word: he would shake his head
with a mocking laugh at the disappointed woman.

(*Winter 1937–8*)

Night

But the windy night, the limpid night
that memory only touches lightly, is remote,
a memory. There exists an astonished calm
made of leaves and nothingness. From that time
beyond memories there only remains a vague
recollection.

               Sometimes that distant astonishment
returns in the daytime, in the motionless light
of a summer sky.

             Through a blank window
the child looked at the night on cool
black hills, surprised to find them
massed together, vague, limpid, motionless. Among the
  leaves
which rustled in the dark, appeared the hills
where all the daytime things, ridges
and trees and vines, were clear and dead
and life was different, made of wind and sky
and leaves and nothingness.

           Sometimes in the
motionless calm of day returns the memory
of that close-knit living in the astonished light.

(*16 April 1938*)

Morning

To Fernanda Pivano

The half-open window frames a face
against the background of the sea. The floating hair
moves to the tender rhythm of the sea.

There are no memories on this face.
Only a fleeting shadow, like a cloud.
The shadow is damp and soft like the sand
in a fresh hollow at dawn.
There are no memories. Only a murmur,
the sea's voice that is now a memory.

In the half-light the slack water of dawn
absorbs the brightness, illumines the face.
Each day a miracle, timeless,
in the sunshine: full of salty light
and the smell of live fish.

There is no memory on this face.
There is no word to contain it
or link it with the past. Yesterday
it vanished from the little window as
a moment vanishes, without sadness
or spoken words, against the background of the sea.

(15–18 August 1940)

Summary (2)

To Fernanda Pivano

There's a small bright garden, between low walls,
full of dry grass and light, its
earth slowly baking. There's a light recalling the sea.
You breathe that grass. A touch on your hair
shakes out its memory.

                    I saw fruit
falling sweet and heavy on grass I remember,
with a plop. You were startled like this
when the blood leapt. You moved your head
as though some miracle of air were happening,
and the miracle is you. There's the same taste
in your eyes and in the warm memory.

                   You listen.
The words you hear hardly touch you.
In your calm face there's a clear thought
weaving the light of the sea around your shoulders.
In your face there's a silence that touches the heart
like the fall of the fruit, and distils an old hurt
like the juice of the fruit as it fell.

(*3–10 September 1940*)

Nocturne

To Fernanda Pivano

The hill is like night against the clear sky.
Your head framed against it, barely moving,
and moving with the sky. You are like a cloud
seen between branches. In your eyes the laughter
and strangeness of a sky that is not yours.

The hill of earth and leaves halts
your bright gaze with its dark mass,
your mouth has the curve of a gentle hollow
between distant slopes. You seem to play
with the great hill and the clearness of the sky:
to please me you echo the ancient background
and make it purer.

       But you live elsewhere.
Your gentle blood came from elsewhere.
The words you say have no meeting-point
with the rugged sadness of this sky.
You are only a white and sweetly gentle cloud
entangled one night among ancient branches.

(*19 October 1940*)

Earth and Death

Red earth, black earth,
you come from the sea,
from the green burnt soil,
with ancient words
and desperate striving
and flowers among the rocks –
you don't know the speech
and striving of the sea you carry,
as rich as memory,
like the bare countryside,
you, like a hard and
deep-sweet word, old in the blood
that gathers in the eyes;
fresh, like fruit
that is memory and season –
you hold your breath
beneath the August sky,
the olives of your glance
can calm the sea,
and you live and live again
without surprise, as firm
as the earth, as dark
as the earth, olive-press
of seasons and dreams
exposed to the moon,
old indeed like
your mother's hands,
the bowl of the brazier.

*

You are like land
that no one has ever talked of.
You expect nothing,
only words
flowing out from the depths
like fruit among the branches.
A wind reaches you.
Dry, twice-dead things
obstruct you and blow away with the wind.
Ancient limbs and words.
You quiver in summer-time.

*

You are also a hill
and a pebble pathway
and a game in the cane-fields,
and you know the vine
which is silent at night.
You say not a word.

There's a silent land,
not your land.
There's a silence which stays
over trees and hills.
There are landscapes and water.
You are a closed silence
which never gives way, you are lips
and dark eyes. You are the vine.

There's a land waiting,
it says no word.
Days have passed
beneath burning skies.
You played with the clouds.

It's poor land –
and your face knows it.
This too is the vine.

I'll find the clouds
and the cane-brake again, the voices
like a moonlight shadow.
I'll find words again
beyond the brief living
of night-time games
and burnt-out childhood.
Silence will be sweet.
You are earth and vine.
A silent flame
will burn up the land
like bonfires in the evening.

*

Your face is carved from stone,
blood from the hard earth,
you came from the sea.
You take all things
and look, and reject them
like the sea. In your heart
you have silence, you swallow
words. You are darkness.
For you dawn is silence.

You are like the voices
of the earth – the clang
of the bucket in the well,
the song of the fire,
the plop of an apple;
the hopeless, muttered

words at the door,
a child's cry – things
that never alter.
You do not change. You are darkness.

You are the closed tavern,
with the bare earth floor,
which the boy once entered
when he had no shoes,
and always remembers.
You are the dark room
he always remembers.
Like the ancient courtyard
where the dawn began.

      *

You do not know the hill
where blood was shed.
So many men escaping,
so many throwing away
their weapons and their names. A woman
watched us go.
Only one among us
stopped with clenched fists,
saw the empty sky,
bowed his head and died, silent,
beside the wall.
Now he's a rag of blood,
just a name. A woman
waits for us on the hills.

      *

Salt water and earth
are in your gaze. One day

you flowed from the sea.
There were trees
beside you, growing warm,
they still remember you.
Aloe and oleander.
All their eyes are closed.
Salt water and earth
are in your veins, your breath.

Warm wind foaming,
shadows of dog-days –
everything closed within you.
You are the hoarse voice
of the countryside, the cry
of hidden quail,
the warmth of a pebble.
The country is weariness,
the country is sorrow.
When night-time comes
peasants are still.
You are the greatest weariness
of the satiating night.

Like rock and grass,
like earth you are closed;
you toss like the sea.
There is no word
which can possess
or stop you. You gather
wounds as the earth does,
give them life, caressing
breath, silence.
You are dried up like the sea,
like a stranded fish,

and you say nothing
and nobody speaks to you.

*

You always come from the sea,
you have its hoarse voice,
always the secret eyes
of running water among brambles,
and a low forehead like
a low cloudy sky.
Each time you live again
like an ancient and
wild thing that the heart
already knew and wanted close.

Each time it's a wrench,
each time it's death.
We always fight.
Whoever chooses hurt
has tasted death
and the gateway to blood.
Like good enemies
whose hate has gone
we have the same
voice, the same pain,
and we face each other
beneath the barren sky.
Between us are no traps,
no useless things –
we shall always fight.

We shall fight again,
we'll always fight,

for we seek the sleep
of death together,
we have hoarse voices,
low foreheads and wildness,
and a matching sky.
We were made for this.
If you or I give way to hurt
a long night follows,
neither peace nor truce
and not real death.
You exist no longer. Arms
struggle in vain.

Until our hearts are shaken.
They have spoken a name for you.
Death begins again.
Unknown wild thing,
you are born again of the sea.

*

And then, cowards that we were,
loving the whisper
of evening, the houses,
the paths along the river,
the red and smudgy lights
from the places there, our grief
softened and unspoken –
we wrenched our hands away
from the living bondage
and were silent, but the blood
leapt in our hearts,
there was no more sweetness,
no more abandonment
to the path along the river –

no longer enslaved, we learnt
to be alone and live.

                *

You are earth and death.
Your season is darkness
and silence. There is no
living thing more distant
from the dawn than you.
When you seem to wake
you are only grief,
grief in your eyes and blood,
but you do not feel. You live
as a stone lives,
like the hard earth.
And dreams clothe you
in sobs that are
unknown to you. Grief
trembles like the water of
a lake, surrounds you.
There are rings on the water.
You let yourself vanish.
You are earth and death.

(*Rome, 1945*)

Two Poems for T.

The trees by the lake
saw you one morning.
Pebbles goats sweat
are outside time,
like the water of the lake.
Grief and the tumult of days
do not ruffle the lake.
The mornings will pass,
sorrow will pass,
other stones and sweat
bite into your blood –
this will not last.
You'll find something again.
There'll come a morning
when, beyond the tumult,
you'll be alone on the lake.

You are also love.
You are made of blood and earth
like others. You walk
like someone who doesn't leave
the door of the house.
You look as though you're waiting
and cannot see. You are earth
that grieves and does not speak.
You know ferment and fatigue,
you have words – you walk
and wait. Love
is your blood – nothing else.

Death Shall Come, Using Your Eyes

To C. from C.

You, dappled smile

You,
dappled smile
on frozen snows –
wind of March,
ballet of boughs
sprung on the snow,
moaning and glowing
your little 'ohs' –
white-limbed doe,
gracious,
would I could know
yet
the gliding grace
of all your days,
the foamlike lace
of all your ways –
tomorrow is frozen
down on the plain –
you, dappled smile,
you, glowing laughter.

(*11 March 1950*)

In the morning you always come back

The gleam of dawn
is the breath from your mouth
at the end of empty streets.
Grey light of your eyes,
sweet drops of dawn
over the dark hills.
Your step and your breath
flood the houses
like the wind of dawn.
The quivering city,
the smell of stone –
you are life, awakening.

Star dispersed
in the light of dawn,
rustle of breeze,
warmth, breath –
the night is over.

You are light and morning.

(*20 March 1950*)

You have blood and breath

You have blood and breath.
You are made of flesh
and hair and looks,
you also. Earth and trees,

light and the sky of March,
quiver, resemble you –
your laughter, your step
like leaping water,
the wrinkle between your eyes
like gathering clouds,
your tender body
like a spot on the sun.

You have blood and breath.
You live on this earth.
You know its flavours,
seasons and awakenings,
you have played in the sun,
you have spoken to us.
Clear water, young shoot
of spring, earth,
germinating silence,
you played as a child
beneath a different sky,
your eyes contain its silence,
a cloud which wells
like a spring from the depths.
Now you laugh and leap
over this silence.
Sweet fruit living
beneath the clear sky,
breathing and living
this season of ours,
in your closed silence
is your strength. Like
live grass you quiver
in the air and smile,
but you are earth.

You are fierce roots.
You are the waiting earth.

(*21 March 1950*)

Death shall come, using your eyes

Death shall come, using your eyes –
the death that is with us
from morning till night, unsleeping,
muted like old remorse
or some foolish vice. Your eyes
will be an empty word,
a cry suppressed, a silence.
Like this each morning you
see it, when you lean alone
over the mirror. O cherished hope,
that day we too shall know
that you are life and nothingness.

Death has a look for everyone.
Death shall come, using your eyes.
It will be like ending a vice,
like seeing a dead face
emerge from the mirror,
like hearing closed lips speak.
We'll go down in silence.

(*22 March 1950*)

You, wind of March

You are life and death.
You came in March
to the bare earth –
your shudder endures.
Blood or spring –
anemone or cloud –
your light step
has raped the earth.
Grief begins again.

Your light step
has awakened grief again.
The earth lay cold
beneath the meagre sky,
lay motionless and closed
in a passive dream
like someone who suffers no more.
Even the frost was sweet
within its deep-lying heart.
Between life and death
hope was silent.

Now every live thing
has speech and blood.
Now earth and sky
are a deep shudder
racked by hope,
upset by morning,
submerged by your step,
your breath of dawn.
Blood of spring,
the whole earth trembles
with an ancient tremor.

You have roused grief again.
You are life and death.
Over the bare earth
you passed as lightly
as swallows or clouds
and the torrent of the heart
awakes, breaks out in violence again
and is mirrored in the sky
and mirrors other things –
those in the sky and the heart
that suffer and twist in grief
as they wait for you.
It is morning, it is dawn,
blood of spring,
you have raped the earth.

Hope is racked with grief
and awaits you, calls you.
You are life and death.
Your step is light.

(25 March 1950)

I shall go through the Piazza di Spagna

The sky will be clear.
The streets will open
below the hills of pine and stone.
No din of the streets will
change this motionless air.
The colour-sprinkled flowers
by the fountains

will look on like women
amused. The steps
the terraces the swallows
will sing in the sun.
That street will open,
the stones will sing,
the heart will beat, leaping
like water in fountains –
this will be the voice
climbing your steps.
The windows will know
the smell of stone and the morning
air. A door will open.
The din of the streets,
the din of the heart,
the light is bewildered.

It will be you – firm and clear.

(*28 March 1950*)

The mornings pass clear

The mornings pass clear
and empty. This way your eyes
were open for a while. The morning
passed slowly, a chasm of
motionless light. It was silent.
Your life was silence; things
lived before your eyes
(no pain no fever no shadow)
like the clear sea in the morning.

You, being light, bring morning.
You will be life, all things.
In you we awoke and breathed
beneath the sky that is still within us.
No pain no fever then
none of that dark shadow from the
scared and different day. O light,
distant brightness, urgent
breath, turn your clear
unmoving eyes on us.
Dark is the morning that passes
without the light of your eyes.

(*30 March 1950*)

The night you slept

Night also resembles you,
distant night that weeps in
silence, deep in the heart,
and the weary stars go by.
One cheek touches another –
a cold shudder, someone
struggles, imploring, lonely
and lost in you, in your fever.

The night suffers, the dawn gasps,
poor heart that leaps up.
O closed face, dark fear,
fever that saddens the stars,
someone who waits for dawn like you

watching your face in silence.
You lie beneath the night
like a closed and dead horizon.
Poor heart that leaps up,
one far-off day you will be dawn.

(*4 April 1950*)

The cats will know

The rain will still fall
on your smooth pavements,
light rain like a
breath of wind or a footstep.
The breeze and the dawn will still
blossom lightly
as though beneath your step,
when you enter again.
Between flowers and window-sills
the cats will know.

There will be other days,
there will be other voices.
You will smile alone.
The cats will know.
You will hear old words,
tired and empty words
like clothes cast off
after yesterday's pleasures.

You will gesture, too.
You will answer with words –

face of springtime,
you will gesture too.

The cats will know,
face of springtime;
the light rain
and the hyacinth-coloured dawn,
breaking the hearts
of those who hope for you no longer,
are the sad smile
which you will smile alone.
There will be other days,
other voices and awakenings.
We shall suffer in the dawn,
face of springtime.

(*10 April 1950*)

Last blues, to be read some day

'Twas only a flirt
you sure did know –
some one was hurt
long time ago.

All is the same
time has gone by –
some day you came
some day you'll die.

Someone has died
long time ago –
some one who tried
but didn't know.

(*11 April 1950*)

Notes

Page 33:

The South Seas This was the opening poem in both the *Solaria* and Einaudi editions of *Lavorare stanca*. It was dedicated to Augusto Monti, the teacher at the Massimo d'Azeglio high school in Turin who, in the words of one of Pavese's biographers, Lorenzo Mondo, 'became teacher of life and literature to a whole generation of anti-fascists'. Pavese remained closely in touch with him all his life.

Page 37:

Fallen Women This poem remained unpublished until 1962.

Page 44:

The Paper-Smokers Italo Calvino describes this poem as 'extremely important because it is Pavese's first political poem (a rare document of this literary genre in the Italy of those years), because it includes many themes which Pavese was to develop later, and because it is a first sketch for the character in *La luna e i falò* [The Moon and the Bonfire] who was called Nuto'.

Page 50:

Landscape I In *The Poet's Craft* (originally Appendix I to *Lavorare stanca*), Pavese analyses this poem in detail, using it as an illustration of his method of writing at that period. 'Pollo' was a nickname of the painter Mario Sturani.

Page 53:

Street Song Pavese mentions this poem in *This Business of Living* in his entry for 5 December 1935. He refers to the fact that the poem embodies 'a fresh preoccupation' with sexual matters 'in the form of vivid descriptions of sensory experiences'.

Page 69:

Mediterranean Italo Calvino states that the friend who 'says little' was the painter Mario Sturani. According to Sturani this poem relates to a summer trip he and Pavese made to Florence, to a Negro they saw at Pisa station and to their stay at Camogli, a fishing-port near Genoa.

Page 71:

Green Wood Italo Calvino writes: 'The title ... recalls the image of smoke, like "The Paper-Smokers", and has clearly the same purpose of indicating Pavese's clear-cut critical attitude towards the immaturity of the clandestine anti-fascist movement; or towards the fate of the anti-fascist youth of Turin who were destined to burn away in jail while still "green".

'The dedication to Massimo (Mila) reminds us of the climate in which the poem was written: Mila had already been in prison once (in 1929), and in 1935 he was arrested again (along with the whole Turin group, including Pavese) and sentenced to seven years' imprisonment (subsequently reduced to two). Mila recalls that as soon as Pavese had written the poem he brought it to him at his home with the dedication; in the 1936 *Solaria* edition of *Lavorare stanca* – which was printed while Mila was in prison – the poem appeared without the dedication; it reappeared in the Einaudi edition of 1943.'

Page 73:

A Generation Italo Calvino believes that this poem was almost certainly written during the same week as the preceding one. When, in 1935, the *Solaria* edition of *Lavorare stanca* was about to be published, Pavese, who was in prison at the time, realized that there would be censorship difficulties. Davide Lajolo quotes in *Il vizio assurdo* (Milan, 1960) a letter written by Pavese from prison on 7 August 1935 to Alberto Carocci, editor of *Solaria*: 'I think that the volume in its final form, with the exception of "Una generazione", could come out now, simply by sending the proofs to the Ministry of the Interior for authorization.'

Page 77:

Revolt Italo Calvino writes: 'This poem probably refers also to an episode of fascist violence. But the link between the death evoked in the first two lines and the character of the beggar in the last lines is not clear. Yet this is perhaps the key to the title: does the beggar embody the ultimate possible form of revolt? The variants in the drafts do not clarify the obscurities.'

Page 80:

Portrait of the Author In this case Italo Calvino believes that the variants in the drafts 'clarify the starting-point of the poem: two vagrants seated on the ground, one without his trousers and one without his pullover, together form a naked body.

'The poem continues by developing the related images of skin–smell–sexual potency, seen by one of the men who identifies himself with the smooth skin, has no smell and sees himself resembling the *ragazzotto* (a word later replaced by the Piedmontese term *gorbetta*) who has "got legs like a snake as well" and is still waiting to pass the test of love. The title and the dedication evidently had humorous associations for the friends to whom Pavese read his poems.'

Page 85:

Grappa in September In his diary Pavese referred on 16 December 1935 to 'one of my poems which consists more simply of images ... ends in fact with the maxim *which unifies all the images:* "Like this the women/won't be the only ones to relish the morning." '

Page 89:

August Moon   On 24 November 1935 Pavese described this poem in his diary as 'the creation of a natural mystery round human anguish'.

Page 93:

Poggio Reale   The title refers to Pavese's detention in the prison of Poggio Reale, in Naples, while in transit to Brancaleone.

Page 96:

Simplicity   'This morning,' Pavese recorded in his diary entry for 17 October 1935, 'I took up again, and finished, the poem about the hare. I had lost heart with it, simply because a hare hardly seemed a worthwhile subject, and I feel a certain self-satisfaction at having persisted in my effort. It really seems to me that my technique has become automatic, so that, without deliberately thinking about it, my ideas now come out in the form of images, as if in obedience to that fanciful law that I mentioned on the 10th. And I am very much afraid that this means it is time to change the tune, or at least the instrument. Otherwise I shall find myself sketching out a critical study of a poem even before I write it. Pure burlesque!'

Page 102:

Deola's Return   Italo Calvino writes: 'From the corrections to the drafts it can be argued that Pavese began this poem about the disillusionment of return in the first person plural with the adjectives in the masculine; the idea of using as a protagonist a prostitute who takes up her former life again probably came to him later, and then the adjectives become feminine and the poem develops the theme of the prostitute; an effort is made to put everything in the third person; then it returns to the third person plural with the adjectives in the masculine and eliminates the more explicit references to the prostitute's life in such a way that – in spite of the title – it seems clear that Pavese is speaking of himself.'

For reasons of clarity, in my English translation of this poem I have used the first person singular rather than the first person plural.

Page 111:

The Drunken Old Woman   On 30 December 1937 Pavese wrote in his diary in more hopeful terms of his recent progress: '. . . again I have sought to express myself in poetry, and succeeded with "The Drunken Old Woman" '.

Page 116:

Morning   Pavese's letters to Fernanda Pivano began at this period and the poem was dedicated to her.

Pages 117 *and* 118:

Summer (2) *and* *Nocturne*   These poems also were dedicated to Fernanda Pivano.

Pages 119–26:

Earth and Death   Italo Calvino writes: 'The verses which Pavese wrote in Rome between 27 October and 3 December 1945 are quite different from his poetic output until five years previously and must be situated in the framework of his other writings at this period of intense production: the atmosphere of Mediterranean mythology is the same as in the *Dialoghi con Leucò* [Dialogues with Leucò] and the novel written in alternate chapters with Bianca Garufi (*Fuoco grande*) [The Great Fire]; the political commitment, which is here expressed in the form of elegiac remorse over those fallen in the struggle, is the same as that defined in the essays and programmatic writings of the period.'

Pavese's diary entries between November and December for this year contain intense self-questioning about love and death. The mythological atmosphere is echoed in one reference to a woman: 'Astarte-Aphrodite-Melita is still sleeping. She will wake in a bad humour.' And on the following day (27 November) Pavese makes reference to the second line of the first poem in the *Earth and Death* sequence, writing 'Aphrodite "came from the sea"'.

In 1949 – following the first publication of this group of poems in the review *Le tre Venezie* (Padua, 1947) – two of the poems, the first and the fifth, were published in the catalogue for an exhibition in Milan of drawings by Ernesto Treccani. The whole group was included also in an anthology of modern Italian poetry published in 1950, *Antologia della poesia italiana 1909–1949*.

Page 127:

Two Poems for T   These remained unpublished until 1962. The 'T' to whom they were dedicated can perhaps, according to Italo Calvino, be identified with the 'Ter.' mentioned in Pavese's diary entry for 25 April 1946: 'Ter. is the usual *aftermath* of your bouts of passion.'

Pages 128–38:

Death Shall Come, Using Your Eyes   The last three of this group of ten poems were probably written in Rome, the rest probably in Turin. The first and last of these – 'You, dappled smile' and 'Last blues, to be read some day' – were written in English by Pavese. The English poem titles, 'In the morning you always come back', 'You, wind of March', 'The night you slept' and 'The cats will know', were Pavese's and appear in English in the Einaudi edition, though the poems themselves were written in Italian. All were addressed to the American film actress Constance Dowling and should be read alongside the last pages of *This Business of Living*. Constance Dowling was killed in a car accident in California two years later.